WHEN REBEL WAS COOL

When Rebel Was Cool: Growing-up in Dixie 1950-1965
Copyright © 2020 by James Ronald Kennedy

ALL RIGHTS RESERVED. No part of this publication may be reproduced, distributed, or transmitted in any form or by any means, including photocopying, recording, or other electronic or mechanical methods, or by any information storage and retrieval system without the prior written permission of the publisher, except in the case of very brief quotations embodied in critical reviews and certain other non-commercial uses permitted by copyright law.

Produced in the Republic of South Carolina by

Shotwell Publishing, LLC
Post Office Box 2592
Columbia, South Carolina 29202

www.ShotwellPublishing.com

Cover Image: Artist Jerry McWilliams

ISBN: 978-1-947660-35-9

10 9 8 7 6 5 4 3 2 1

WHEN REBEL WAS COOL

Growing-up in Dixie 1950-1965

JAMES RONALD KENNEDY

SHOTWELL PUBLISHING
COLUMBIA, SOUTH CAROLINA

Contents

Chapter 1:
When My Memories Began 1

Chapter 2:
Growing Up in the Bible Belt 11

Chapter 3:
School Days in Dixie. 21

Chapter 4:
Breakfast in the Rural South 25

Chapter 5:
After-School Snacks 29

Chapter 6:
Taking Guns to School 33

Chapter 7:
Our Chores: Working the Farm 39

Chapter 8:
Which Is Better: Man's Wealth or God's Wealth. . . . 47

Chapter 9:
The War and the Origin of the Bible Belt. 55

Chapter 10:
Our Family Remembered the War 61

Chapter 11:
Uncle Frank Smith:
Snake Handler and Country Philosopher 67

Chapter 12:
LOGGING WITH OX TEAMS 75

Chapter 13:
HOG-KILLING TIME:
MEAT FOR SUPPER RAISED ON THE FARM 79

Chapter 14:
PLOWING THE RED CLAY HILLS OF MISSISSIPPI 85

Chapter 15:
THE DINNER BELL: THE COMMUNITY'S 911 CALL 91

Chapter 16:
THE OLE SWIMMING HOLE:
DAYS BEFORE SWIMMING POOLS 95

Chapter 17:
MOVING A TOWN ON OX WAGONS 99

Chapter 18:
TV COMES TO THE RURAL SOUTH 103

Chapter 19:
STARVATION — THE HUNGRY SOUTH 109

Chapter 20:
SICKNESS AND DISEASE IN THE SOUTH 115

Chapter 21
PHOTOS 121

Chapter 22:
MAKING DO IN HARD TIMES 133

Chapter 23:
RACE RELATIONS IN THE RURAL SOUTH 143

Chapter 24:
HOWARD DIVINITY:
COPIAH COUNTY'S BLACK CONFEDERATE 155

Chapter 25:
HOW TO SPEAK SOUTHERN:
REDNECK WORDS AND PHRASES 159

Chapter 26:
EPILOGUE: THOUGHTS IN THE QUIET OF TWILIGHT 199

Chapter 1:

WHEN MY MEMORIES BEGAN

Typical Southern farmer in 1947 when the Kennedy Twins were born. Photo courtesy Library of Congress (LOC).

The past is never dead; it is not even past.
— William Faulkner

THIS BOOK IS WRITTEN FOR the benefit of my grandchildren, my twin brother's and our older brother's grandchildren, and all the grandchildren of the South. I wanted to tell the stories of my personal experiences growing up in the rural South from 1950 to 1965. Actually, they are the experiences of the Kennedy Twins—Donald and I lived these accounts, and often, I am *at a loss* as to whether I remember something, or I just remember him talking about an incident he remembers. These stories, and photographs—some over 100 years old and in poor condition—are our stories written for our grandchildren and all the grandchildren of the South, even if they no longer live in the South. One day, our grandchildren may want to know why their grandfathers loved the South so much, especially during a time when the leftwing secular world is actively engaged in destroying Confederate monuments and viciously slandering the honor of the men who wore the gray in the War for Southern Independence—the correct name for the so-called *Civil War*. I hope and pray that one day our grandchildren and other Southern grandchildren will read these accounts, otherwise, they will never know the truth—a truth that sadly, today, is not allowed to be publicly told. The truth about our South that is vigorously censored in a nation that claims to be the "land of the free."

In 1950, my twin brother, Donald, and I turned three. It was around this time that our memories of growing up in *Dixie* began. By the time we left home in 1965 at the age of eighteen, we had witnessed a great change in the rural South. In the years since 1965, the South has continued to change, but it still remains uniquely Southern. I am not the same as I was back in 1950 when my memories began, but I am still the same person; grown, matured, wisdom gained from happy and sad experiences, and educated with two master's degrees from well-known Universities, yet I am still me. The same is true for our Southern homeland; it is not the same as it was in 1950, but it is still the South, or *Dixie* as we sometimes call the South. This is the story these simple pages will tell; a story of my personal experiences watching and being a part of the South's growth, its triumph over poverty, disease, and its endurance over slander and lies. It is the story of my homeland, a land sanctified by the blood of heroes and the land in whose tender arms sleep the earthly remains of my ancestors. It is a land and a people

Southern Sugar

NORTHERN SUGAR

(Artwork Charles Hayes)

that I defend because I believe, as did Native American Chief Joseph of the Nez Perce tribe, "A man who would not love his father's grave is worse than a wild animal."

While reading this book, you will come across Southern words and phrases that you may find to be unfamiliar. Throughout the text, I have italicized words and phrases that may be unfamiliar. These italicized words and phrases, plus many others, are listed at the end of the book in a chapter entitled "How to Speak Southern." Some may call it a "Red Neck Dictionary."

This book is a grouping of stories about incidents in our lives that occurred in the fifteen years from 1950 to 1965. These stories are written in a form of free-flowing text or stream of consciousness. There are underlying themes and subthemes, but no story line as in a novel. For example, I may begin to explain what *corn pone* is and take a divergence and begin to discuss what at first seems to be unrelated to the discussion of *corn pone*. Bear with me as we take these side trips — they are important and they do relate, especially to the book's theme and subthemes.

This book's primary theme is that while Yankees get their history from textbooks written by Yankees to glorify Yankee heroes and ideas, Southerners get their history from our family. Over and over again I stress that the victor writes the official history. The Yankee victor, not satisfied with merely writing the official history, uses his military, economic, and political power to enforce his version of history. But the invaded, conquered, and occupied nation (the South) also has its version of history — the defeated and occupied nation's version is recorded as oral history and passed down generation by generation as stories told to each other in small family gatherings around the *supper* table and at family reunions.

This book's primary and secondary themes play out within the context of a society — the rural South. The rural South (1950-1965) was a society that was spiritually rich but materially impoverished. Post War Yankees reconstructed, as in remade, the South into a society more in fitting with what they thought we deserved. The antebellum South — often referred to in this book as the pre-War South — was a prosperous South. But *the War*, occupation, and the cruel manner in which emancipation (ending slavery) was accomplished destroyed the formerly rich South. Yankee enforced emancipation and war was a cruel process that turned the South into a land of massive poverty. The victors remade the pre-War prosperous South into the post-War impoverished South. This poverty was intentionally inflicted upon black and white people of the South by our conquering masters. In describing the conditions of the impoverished South, I often make references to "Yankees." Yankees would include anyone who does not live in one of the sixteen Southern states. Southerners who have moved up North are not Yankees. They are displaced Southerners. Southerners who were forced by poverty to leave home in search of a way out of Yankee induced poverty, but taking with them their Southern folkways, customs, food, and accents.

The old folks, when discussing the trials and tribulations of *the War* — such as the destruction to private property and the death of civilians caused by the likes of Yankee General Sherman — would often use the term Damn-Yankee (said as if it were one word, not two). I refrain from using such label because today there are many Northerners, especially in the plains and mountains of the West, who come from a farming or ranching background, who are traditionally conservative in their social policies and who have a sense of community and patriotism similar to the traditional South. There is also a growing number of Northerners who, when viewing the degeneration of America's social, political, and spiritual values, have come to the conclusion that the South was right! Right, at least, with regard to our traditional insistence upon a limited government with strong states' rights to enforce the limitations placed upon the Federal government by the original Constitution.

Mrs. Douglas, family friend, Mom and Dad in our kitchen, circa 1963.

This book is a collection of personal memories. Memories of growing up in the rural South, in the poorest state in the Union, a state that once was among the richest states in the Union — the once sovereign state of Mississippi. But the underlying theme holds true regardless of what Southern state we might consider. While the geography of the red clay hills of Mississippi is radically different from the geography of the mountains of North Carolina, the principles, maintained by the book's theme, remains constant. I endeavor to use personal experiences to demonstrate that while

When My Memories Began

Yankees get their history from history books written by Yankees to glorify Yankee ideas and heroes—Southerners get their history from their family. These family histories regarding the so-called *Civil War*—referred to in this book as the War for Southern Independence or simply *the War*—were impacted by the fact that beginning in the mid-1950s, the South was celebrating *the War's* centennial. Every white school child wanted to know if his grandfather or great grandfather rode with the Confederate Gray Ghost (Colonel John Singleton Mosby) or served under General Robert E. Lee. It was a time before cell phones and the internet. It was an era when young and old would spend time talking to each other. Great stories were told and thereby passed down to our generation. Oral history is important in the preservation of a people's knowledge and understanding of themselves, their unique society, and their special place in the world at large. Storytelling is an important aspect of social continuity, and Southerners, after all, are great storytellers.

One of the many dichotomies or contradictions of our Southern society is created by the fact that our society is composed of two major races—black and white. While the white South was celebrating the *Civil War* centennial, the black South was beginning the push for equality under the law via the Civil Rights movement. During these times, neither side understood the other—which was one of the greatest tragedies of that era. From reading personal accounts of former slaves and accounts of whites who lived through *the War*—I believe black and white Southerners understood each other better during *the War* than we did a hundred years later. It took a great deal of sacrifice on the part of the black South before all Southerners came to accept, endorse, and defend the principle of equality under the law. Unfortunately, many today look upon the South's celebration of its heroes of the War for Southern Independence as part of the resistance to black Civil Rights. Such an assessment is incorrect. I have no doubt that many misguided white folks in the South tried to link the two for their own political benefit, but any linkage was only a linkage against the Federal government—the same Federal government that our blood relatives fought against during *the War*.

This dichotomy in the Southern society has been with us from the beginning, even before the United States became an independent country. During the days of slavery, it was impossible for Yankees to understand that, even though slaves did not appreciate enslavement, these same slaves, for the most part, did not hate white Southerners. How can this be? It is a mystery that Southerners back in the day did not try to explain, they merely accepted it. It is a wonderful example of how black Southerners could endure and eventually overcome the oppressions of slavery while maintaining the spirit of Christian charity and sense of kith and kin for their white neighbors. It serves as an object lesson for all to see. It is an inspiration to see how the black South could spend three hundred years nailed to the cross of slavery and yet remain charitable toward the white society they served. Most people today cannot understand this, but I can understand it! I understand it because I have an advantage over most Americans living today—an advantage I want to share with you.

I personally witnessed another similar Southern dichotomy. I lived through the "long hot summers" of the Civil Rights movement in the South. I recall the violence and hatred that emerged from the efforts of black Southerners to rid our society of legally enforced racial segregation. By the mid to late 1950s, it suddenly became evident to white Southerners that black Southerners hated racial segregation. Believe it or not, this came as a surprise to most of the white South. After all, racial segregation was inherited by the generation of the 1950s—it was the way things had always been. I am sure that this was also the thinking of white Southerners back in the days of slavery; they did not create the system of slavery; they merely inherited the system of slavery; and after all (from their vantage point) this was the way it has always been. That was the way it was for the generations before the War, and so it was with the generation of white Southerners of the 1950s.

Southerners are, by nature, traditionalists. We are quick to adopt or create useful traditions, but we are also very slow to change long established traditions—even when it becomes evident that the tradition is no longer socially useful. Our society is not set in stone, we do allow our society to change, but change must come slowly over a great length of time. This is the exact opposite of the rushed pace of change in Yankee society—which is one more source for friction between the North and South. We have a faith set in the absolute values of Holy Scripture; therefore, our social values that were developed over generations of trial and error, must not be quickly discarded. Southerners have a saying that one must be careful not to throw the baby out with the bath water. Social change must be based upon more than just having a desire to improve society (good intentions). Human history has taught us that there is a better guide than human reason. We do not reject reason, but history has taught us that human reason must be tempered, or else society will fall prey to every emotional "ism" dreamed up by some ideological fanatic (social justice warriors, etc.) whose primary purpose is to obtain the power to force society to accept an untried and untested political ideology. The dead bodies piled up by twentieth century "isms" of Nazism, Fascism, Socialism, and Communism stand as mute witnesses to the validity of the tradition-loving South's reluctance to join mass movements of social radicalism. Thus, the Southern people's reluctance to join the mass, politically correct, hysteria promoting "progressive" "isms" such as feminism, globalism, and various forms of isms promoting what our Christian based, moral standards would call sexual perversions.

The post-War impoverishment of the South created an additional problem for the people of the post-War South with which pre-War Southerners never had to deal. Unlike their prosperous pre-War (antebellum) counterparts, impoverished rural Southerners were primarily concerned with putting food on the table, clothes on their backs, and keeping a roof over their heads. Providing the basic necessities of life consumed the majority of their existence. They did not have the luxury of spending endless hours studying and debating social justice issues of the day. Before you condemn Southern people of a by gone era, try first to put yourself in their shoes. But here is a caution that must be understood: You will never be able to put yourself in their shoes if the only history you know is the history written and enforced by the victors in the War for Southern Independence.

But, back to the dichotomy of the 1950s. Despite black Southerner's hatred for the system of racial segregation, they did not hate their white neighbors. Black Southerners struggling under Jim Crow (government enforced racial segregation) in the 1950s reacted in a manner similar to black Southerners struggling under the weight of slavery in the 1850s. In this book, I use personal accounts to demonstrate how close and friendly black and white Southerners were during this turbulent time of change and growth. That closeness was in everything except politics. Today, this closeness remains in many places, but the one great divide is in the political arena. Donald and I discussed this in our last two books. It is a technique used by all empires to control an occupied people—the technique is called "divide and rule."

Jim Crow segregation, just like slavery, could not destroy the sense of kith and kin that had developed over the centuries between all Southerners regardless of skin color. But race is not the only thing, or even the primary thing discussed in this book. The reader will get a window into the past, and as you look through this window, you will see a world you never knew, but a world that is part of your history.

The photographs of Southern sharecroppers were taken in the late 1930s. Did these Southerners have more in common with each other than they did with the finical elite on Wall Street and the political elite in Washington, D.C.? And today—what about their descendants? Yet, today, politics divides us, but who benefits from this political division?

A Word About Slavery And Racial Segregation

The enemies or critics of the South use slavery and racism as a magic wand to dispel all attempts to say or write good things about the South. Slavery and racism (white supremacy and racial segregation) are used by the South's enemies as a smokescreen behind which to hide their evil intentions, both past and present. With great self-conceit, and arrogance, they boastfully pronounce the South as evil by claiming that "slavery (pre-War) or racial segregation (post-War) would still be legal today if the North had not forced the South to surrender such evils." They use their political, financial, and social dominance to enforce their made-up narrative of what life would have been like had they not intervened and freed the slaves or destroyed *Jim Crow* racial segregation. They claim that had it not been for the sacrifices of the virtuous North, slavery or racial segregation would still exist today in the South. But they do not have a crystal ball that tells them what would have happened had the South been allowed to continue as a free and independent nation. Why should their narrative—the invader's narrative—be accepted as fact? They can maintain their narrative only as long as they maintain their dominance; only as long as they can prevent an alternative narrative from being offered. They can maintain their control of our society only as long as they can continue to censor the truth about why they invaded the South and waged a genocidal war against their former countrymen.

Before *the War* Senator Jefferson Davis (Democrat, Mississippi) gave a speech in the U.S. Senate encouraging the nation to follow what he called "the high road to emancipation." He and most Southerners wanted to find a way to end slavery. As Confederate General Robert E. Lee declared before *the War*, "slavery is an inherent evil in any society." The South understood this and was, at one time, the leader in the American movement to abolish slavery. Up to the 1830s, there were more abolition societies in the South than in the North! What happened? The North rejected peaceful abolition of slavery and adopted radical abolition. The North began demanding immediate and uncompensated emancipation, even if it were done by a massive slave revolt in which white Southerners—slave owners and non-slave owners alike—would be slaughtered. Northern radical abolitionists' interference in the South's quest for the "high road to emancipation" effectively halted the emancipation movement in the South.

White supremacy and racial segregation began up North and were imported down South. As a captive nation, the South has been unable to defend itself against unending Yankee slander. Victorious

Yankees made the South the North's scapegoat for America's sin of slavery and racism—leaving the guilty party with the façade of innocence. Donald and I discuss this unnatural *cultural distortion* of Southern society caused by Yankee interference, and eventual invasion, conquest, and occupation of the South in "Punished With Poverty-the Suffering South" and "Yankee Empire: Aggressive Abroad and Despotic at Home."

Sharecropping — A New Form of Slavery — It Lasted Until 1965

Southern sharecropper children circa 1930s. Courtesy Library of Congress (LOC)

Young Southerner picking cotton, circa 1935. (Photo Wikimedia Commons).

Chapter 2:

GROWING UP IN THE BIBLE BELT

THE SOUTH IS KNOWN by many titles, such as: *Dixie*, Beulah Land, the Confederate States of America, the Sun-Belt, the Pine Belt, and the *Bible Belt*. The title of *Bible Belt* best describes the Southern people's traditional Christian faith. There are more churches per person in the South than any other region of the United States. Church attendance in the South is far higher than church attendance in New England or other Northern states. For example; a recent poll documented that 75% of the people in the Southern state of Mississippi believe with absolute certainty in the existence of God, whereas only 43% of the people in the New England State of Massachusetts believe with absolute certainty in the existence of God. There is, and always has been, a major difference in the spiritual values of the people in the South and other sections of the U.S.A.

Church attendance was a major part of growing up in *Dixie* for the Kennedy Twins. The non-religious and anti-Christian people in Hollywood, the liberal media, and neo-Marxist university professors use the label *Bible Belt* as if it were a curse. They use it against the South in an attempt to humiliate and insult Southerners, but we accept the label as a badge of honor. As Mom (Linnie Mae Berry Kennedy,1917-2006) used to tell us, "If Satan is angry with you, then you must be doing something right."

Typical rural Southern church 1950s.
Photo courtesy Library of congress (LOC).

Mom and Dad (Burnice Edgar Kennedy 1909-1988) made sure our "upbringing" included firm instructions about our need for salvation through an acceptance of Jesus Christ as our Lord and Savior and encouraged us to live a life that would serve as evidence of our Christian faith. In 1951 Dad was ordained a Deacon of Pearl Valley Baptist Church and Mom was a Sunday School teacher. Prayer and Bible reading was a major part of our family life. I can well remember Dad reading his Bible while sitting in front of the fireplace during the winter months with wood logs slowly burning down for the night. The fireplace, at the time, was the only form of heating in the house. Looking back, I now see that we were typical of rural, *Bible Belt* families of that time.

Our local Baptist Church (Pearl Valley) was like most small rural churches in the South at that time — it was too poor to afford an inside baptistry. When someone makes a formal profession of faith in Jesus and joins a Baptist Church, they will be baptized via immersion. Baptism, in our church, was done the same way it had been done in the South for generations — in a creek, river, or lake. Peggy Creek ran on the backside of our forty-five-*acre* farm (Peggy Creek was named after a Choctaw woman). It emptied into the Pearl River several miles to the east. The Church had a special place on the banks of Peggy Creek, where all the baptisms were held. The creek's water was spring fed, and the creek, at that time, had trees on both banks all along its course that kept the sun's warming rays away from the cold water. I remember wading out into that cold water and waiting for my turn to be baptized by our minister, "Brother Bullard." I recall the congregation standing on the creek bank singing "Shall We Gather at the River," and "On Jordan's Stormy Banks I Stand." Even though most of the members of that small congregation are now in Heaven, the connection is still there — a tie that binds us all together; those of us left here on earth and our Heavenly family of *kith and kin* now in Heaven awaiting the day when we too shall join their Heavenly numbers.

When the young people in our church became teenagers and the older ones had driving licenses, it was a common thing for us to get together during the summer and attend revival meetings (church services held during the week) in neighboring communities. It gave us an opportunity to visit with young people from neighboring communities. Without realizing it, we were also absorbing a lot of Christian teaching. We visited both Baptist and Methodist churches — in rural Mississippi of the time, Methodist and Baptist were the primary churches.

In the early 1960s, many church members across the South still referred to their Revival Meetings as their Annual Protracted Meeting. In the old days, even prior to our youth, churches would hold annual "all day preaching, singing and *dinner* on the ground" after the crops were *laid by*. This usually happened in mid-June to mid-July in our part of the South. Once crops are *laid by*, the work in the field is over, and the farmer has free time to do other chores and attend church meetings until it is time to harvest the crops—usually beginning in August and running through the fall. To modern urban people who seldom walk off concrete or asphalt, it may seem unusual that people would spend so much time going to church. But agrarian people (farmers and ranchers) understand their complete dependency on nature and, therefore, nature's God for the success of their farms and ranches. Being close to the soil and close to Mother Nature will naturally produce a people who can more readily see themselves as dependent upon God for their survival. The artificial environment in "modern" urban areas tend to hide or mask man's natural dependency upon nature's God.

The social impact that religious training and upbringing had on the people of the South was demonstrated to Donald and I in the early 1960s. Our Dad had contracted to paint a house near Wesson, Mississippi. Of course, during the summer months, we were expected to work alongside of our father—he taught us early the value of money earned by hard work. We did not know the family who lived in the house we were painting, but they were typical of Southern families of the day. Each morning, the lady of the house would leave with breakfast food, soap, wash cloth, and towel. After an hour or so, she would return. At noon, she would leave, taking more food with her and again in the afternoon just prior to us leaving around sundown. After a couple of days observing the lady's activities, curiosity overcame us, and we asked Dad what was she doing. Dad responded, "She is taking care of Jesus." Well, Donald and I were pretty sure that Jesus did not live down a rural road in Mississippi, so with perplexed looks, we asked Dad what he meant. He then quoted Jesus from the scriptures (which he was good at doing), "Matthew 25:40; In-as-much as ye have done it unto one of the least of these my brethren, ye have done it unto me." He then explained to us that there was an elderly black lady who lived all alone down the road. The black lady had always been a friend of this family. She was now very sick and would soon pass away, but the black lady had no relatives living close by to help take care of her. So, her white friend was ministering to this black lady in her final days upon this earth. And Dad reminded us to pray for her because "there is no color difference in our souls."

Shortly after the Kennedy Twins were baptized in Peggy Creek, Brother Bullard graduated from Mississippi (Baptist) College and moved on to another church. We were very lucky to have a new preacher who was also one of our school teachers at Wesson Elementary School. Most ministers of small rural Southern churches had to have a second

Photo of Brother Douglas preaching from pulpit at Pearl Valle Baptist Church circa 1970.

source of income, and many were teachers. This was a blessing in disguise because it put a number of men in teaching roles. The impact of male teachers upon young boys cannot be overestimated. Our new pastor was Rev. Martin Luther Douglass (1921-1990) — or Brother Douglas, as we all would call him. He was a World War II veteran and would tell us about his adventures with the Army Air Corps (this is what the Air Force was called while it was still attached to the Army). During the summer, he would take time off from family affairs to organize swimming outings for the young people of the church. While he was certainly a great preacher, delivering many a well-thought-out and prayed-up sermon each Sunday, his dedication to the Lord was expressed in one of his favorite sayings from the Bible, "Faith without works is dead." Brother Douglas put his faith to work by the way he used his free time to keep young people busy with wholesome activities. He also worked to help neighbors in times of need. I recall a time when a family lost everything in a house fire. Many people came by and told the man of the house to "let me know if I can help." But Brother Douglas came to the scene, loaded the children into his car, took the children to town, and bought them all shoes because they had lost all their shoes in the fire. Words are important, but action demonstrates the sincerity of easily spoken words.

At school, Brother Douglas very patiently encouraged the Kennedy Twins to be more diligent in our studies — I am sure he must have felt that he was a failure when it came to encouraging the Kennedy Twins to "apply yourself to your studies." He encouraged us to reach beyond our limited horizons. I recall how he sat us down and told us that if we improved our studies, we could go to college and major in political science! We had no idea they taught such things. But, like so many Southern children of the time, our parents could not afford the cost of sending one of us, let alone both of us, to college. Once again, Brother Douglas came to the rescue by helping us gain admittance to what was then a vocational training called Inhalation Therapy (now Respiratory Therapy) taught at Baptist Hospital in Jackson, Mississippi. That modest beginning would set two simple country boys on a lifetime of educational excellence and professional careers. During our professional careers we have tried to repay Brother Douglas' kindness by doing similar things for young people, especially those who we employed to work under us in our professional careers.

Books were considered a luxury in our home. Books cost money, and money was always in short supply. This resulted in there being very few books in our home other than personal Bibles. Every family member had a Bible, and we faithfully took our Bibles to Church and Sunday School every Sunday. Each quarter, the Sunday School would purchase new Sunday School "books" (actually, no more than paper brochures) for all Sunday School students. These Sunday School books were published by the Southern Baptist Convention. During the week, we would read the upcoming Sunday School lesson. One Baptist Sunday School "book" made a definite impact on the Kennedy Twins. It arrived sometime during the late 1950s or early 1960s. It contained typical Sunday School lessons written under the guidance of the Southern Baptist Convention. On the back of this particular Sunday School "book" was a photograph of General Robert E. Lee's monument in Dallas, Texas. Beneath the photograph of Lee's monument was one of General Lee's famous quotes: "Duty then is the most sublime word in the English language. Do your duty in all things, you cannot do more and you should never wish to do less." When we completed studying that quarter's Sunday School book, before discarding the "book," Donald and I cut off the back page with the photo of General Lee's monument with the quote, and pinned it to the wall of our room. There it remained for years—how I wish we had kept a copy of that Baptist Sunday School "book." At that time, we never would have believed that the day would come when the Southern Baptist Convention would "bear false witness" against our dead Confederate ancestors and those of us who understand the truth about why that war was fought. The Southern Baptist Convention did this in a convulsion of political correctness by associating Southern heritage with racism and banning the display of Confederate flags in cemeteries where Confederate veterans are buried.

In our current secular humanist society, it has become common to tear down monuments to men like General Lee. Evil, ungodly men have falsely accused General Lee of being a racist who endorsed and fought to maintain human slavery ("bearing false witness"). Yet, the truth is exactly opposite—Lee and most Southerners of his generation had a high regard for their fellow Southerners regardless of skin color. As previously noted, even the modern day Southern Baptist Convention has fallen into the trap of "hate Southern heritage and slander those who honor their Southern heritage." It is a trap set by secular humanists who want to destroy all traditional American values, not just traditional Southern values. Secular humanists view our Southern heritage as an easy <u>first</u> target or "low hanging fruit." It is sad to realize that we live in an age when Christian churches are blindly falling for this secular humanist trap and slandering the dead and those of us who wish to honor our dead. Too many "modern" churches are blindly bearing false witness against their Southern neighbors—men and women of the South who respect their ancestors who wore the gray in the War for Southern Independence. These churches, in their historical ignorance, slander their neighbors who have carefully studied *the War* and understand the truth as to why Lincoln and his comrades invaded, conquered, viciously slandered, and exploited the South. These churches think they are right, and their intentions, while misguided, are good, but the road to hell is paved with misguided, good intentions. If only they would take the time to learn the truth that the invader has purposely hidden from them.

Rosa Parks circa 1955.
(Photo Wikipedia Commons).

General Lee wrote to his wife before *the War* that slavery was an evil in any society. He gladly freed (emancipated) the slaves owned by his wife's father, who had left it in his will that his slaves were to be freed—Lee carried out his father-in-law's wishes during *the War*! Shortly after the end of *the War*, General Lee was attending church in Richmond, Virginia. When the minister gave the altar call, a black man rose and came down the aisle, and knelt at the altar. The white congregation did not know what to do—this was a new time, and no one was certain about the black man's intention. There was an uneasy stillness in the church, no one moved until General Lee rose, walked down the aisle, and knelt beside the black man. Soon, the altar was crowded. This is the character of the man that evil secular humanists (and misguided churches) are slandering and attempting to censor from Southern society. Today, too many mainline churches, out of

Growing Up in the Bible Belt

ignorance, fear, or malice, are actively bearing false witness against not only General Robert E. Lee but all Southerners who honor the truth about our Southern heritage.

A major scene of the Southern Civil Rights Movement occurred in 1955 when a black lady, Rosa Parks, refused to move from a seat in the "white only" section of a public bus in Montgomery, Alabama. When told to move, she refused and was arrested. This was not the first time a Southern lady had been arrested for failing to obey racial segregation (*Jim Crow*) laws that were used to enforce separate accommodations for black and white people.

On the evening of June 13, 1902, an elderly white lady boarded a streetcar in Alexandria, Virginia. She was tired and encumbered with several packages. The streetcar conductor informed her that she was seated in a section set aside for black folks according to the new racial segregation laws. The lady refused to move even after a black man entered the car and took his place in the "black only" section. The conductor called the police, who arrested the lady. They were embarrassed to find out that they had arrested Mary Custis Lee, the only surviving daughter of General Robert E. Lee!

This incident is important because it shows how General Lee raised his children. Racial segregation was not a "Southern thing" before, during, and for almost fifty years after *the War*. People find it shocking and almost impossible to believe that these laws originated up North. Most Southerners who grew up in the *Bible Belt* were taught from childhood to "do unto others as you would have them do unto you." Southerner children grew up singing in Sunday School "Jesus loves the little children, all the children of the world, red and yellow, black and white, all are precious in His sight." Such training makes it hard, if not impossible, to hate people because of their skin color. It also helped to create a society in which it was possible, perhaps not easy but possible, to correct political errors of the past. Past political errors would include slavery

Mary Custis Lee, 1914. (Photo LOC).

and government enforced racial segregation. The South's religious training also made it possible for the white South to boldly accept these corrections, and earnestly incorporate these changes into our society, and thus, make a better Southern society.

In 1960, President Dwight D. Eisenhower sent a letter to an individual who questioned why he had kept a photograph of General Robert E. Lee (in Confederate military uniform) in his office while Eisenhower was president. In his letter dated August 9, 1960, replying to the inquiry, President Eisenhower wrote that:

> "General Robert E. Lee was, in my estimation, one of the supremely gifted men produced by our Nation. He believed unswervingly in the Constitutional validity of his cause ... Through all his many trials, he remained selfless almost to a fault and unfailing in his faith in God ... he was noble as a leader and ... unsullied as I read the pages of our history ... a nation of men of Lee's caliber would be unconquerable in spirit and soul ... Such are the reasons that I proudly display the picture of this great American on my office wall."

An American President could not causally write such honorable words about a Confederate soldier today—General Lee's character has not changed—America's character has changed—and changed for the worse.

During the hot debates over slavery prior to *the War* and again during the hot debates over racial segregation laws that occurred during the Civil Rights struggle, white Southerners would plead to the point of begging, "Leave us alone, and let us solve our own problems." The push back from the South was not based upon race as much as it was based upon anger at the hypocritical North that would not allow the South to resolve its social issues on its own slowly over time. Today, most Americans think that segregation (white supremacy) was something established by the South, but in reality, it was something already established in the North and then, after *the War*, imported from the North. During *the War*, Yankee General "Beast" Butler established "Black Codes" in occupied Louisiana. His Black Codes were based upon similar laws then in effect in his home state of Massachusetts. Most Americans incorrectly think that slavery was strictly a Southern issue, but in reality, it was an American issue—the North being primarily responsible for slavery in America. Very few folks know that slavery lasted 75 years longer in Massachusetts than it did in Mississippi. To *add insult to injury*—Massachusetts and other Northern states earned much of their wealth from their involvement in the African slave trade and then enacted exclusion laws to prevent free blacks from coming into their states! But when you lose a war, it is the winners who get to write and enforce their version of history. Yet, while Northerners learn their history from history books written by Northerners to glorify Northern heroes and ideas (and to hide Northern crimes), Southerners learn their history from their family. Our history is family history passed down generation to generation. In our veins flows the blood of our ancestors who wore the gray in the War for Southern Independence. It is our duty to see to it that the truth of our history lives on generation to generation.

A Prayer For Our Enemies—1861.

The prayer below was first printed in Charleston, SC, in 1861—the first year of *the War*. It demonstrates the spirit of a people fighting for their freedom against an evil enemy who has overwhelming power and resources at its command.

> O GOD, we beseech Thee, forgive and pardon our enemies, and give us that measure of Thy grace, that for their hatred we may love them; for their cursing we may bless them; for their injury we may do them good; and for their persecution we may pray for them.
>
> They have laid a net for our steps, and they have digged a pit before us; Lord, we desire not that they themselves should fall into the midst of these, but we beseech Thee keep us out of them, and deliver, establish, bless and prosper us for Thy mercy's sake in Jesus Christ our Saviour, to whom with Thee and the Holy Spirit, we desire to consecrate ourselves and our country, now and forever, imploring Thee to be our GOD, and to make us Thy people. Amen.

As General Beauregard, CSA, declared, "The Federal troops came as invaders, and the Southern troops stood as defenders of their homes."

Empires never invade a free people to improve the condition of the invaded people. Southern children working the field – picking cotton – with their parents circa 1930. Approximately 75 years after the North's glorious victory. Vae Vectus – woe to the vanquished. (Photo LOC).

Chapter 3:

SCHOOL DAYS IN DIXIE

THE KENNEDY TWINS were six years old in the fall of 1953. The school system in Mississippi did not have a Kindergarten system, so we began our public education in the first grade. The school was located in the small village of Rockport. Rockport was originally located on the banks of the Pearl River, but when the G M & O Railroad (Gulf Mobile and Ohio Railroad) established a line close to the old river port, the town was moved about two miles west of the river where the railroad depot was located. The Rockport school house was used for grades 1 through 8. Grades 9 through 12 went to Georgetown High School located another 15 miles north of Rockport, also close to the Pearl River and G M & O Railroad.

The Rockport school house had three classrooms, an auditorium, and a cafeteria. The principle, Mr. Hamilton — our cousin on Dad's side of the family — taught grades 6th, 7th, and 8th; his wife, Mrs. Hamilton, taught 3rd, 4th, and 5th; and, a neighbor, Mrs. Hays, taught 1st and 2nd grades. During morning recess, students, even 1st and 2nd graders, were allowed to walk about one quarter of a mile up the road to the general store — no adult supervision was needed! Needless to say, everyone knew each other, their immediate and extended families. No need for parent teacher conferences in those days. Corporal punishment (paddling) was allowed — this was rarely required

Rockport School House circa 1950. Photo from: Mississippi Department of Archives and History (MDAH).

and then only for a few of the boys. When word got back home that a son had been paddled at school—the father would administer a real thrashing! Why a second whipping? Because the son had embarrassed the family. The decision of teachers was always upheld by the family. Such strict adherence to authority figures made for a generally civil and polite grouping of youngsters and civility among the adults.

There were no indoor facilities for basketball—no gym. Basketball goal posts were set-up on level ground for boys and girls. A large swing set with four to six swings and one large slide was the only formal outdoor equipment. At recess, the boys generally headed to the woods to build forts and play with pretend guns made from the forks of small trees—typically sweet-gum saplings (young trees three to four feet high). One girl, who loved horses, would bring her toy horses and make corrals on the ground and invite us to play horses with her—which I did as often as I could. She would eventually teach

Wesson Elementary School circa 1960. (Photo from MDAH).

me how to ride a horse—she was the first real cowgirl I knew. The boys and girls in the community would spend many a day during the summer riding our horses up and down community roads and in the woods.

In addition to not having indoor basketball facilities, the school did not have indoor restrooms! Girls' and boys' outhouses were the only restroom facilities available. But not too many of us had indoor plumbing at that time so it did not seem strange to use an outhouse.

It always seemed unfair to us boys that the girls' outhouse had a nice sawdust walkway to it. This improvement was important during the winter when it often rained and the dirt paths became wet and muddy. The pathway to the boys' outhouse had a simple dirt pathway, and yes, it became very muddy during the winter.

Dinner time (now days referred to as *lunch*-time) for the first few years of schooling at Rockport consisted of such delicacies as *hominy* and home-grown vegetables with water to drink. The second or third year saw a great improvement as far as we were concerned, no more hominy and the state provided milk — *sweet milk* (white milk) or chocolate milk.

The three classrooms were fitted with simple blackboards — which were actually old slate boards — and a carefully monitored supply of white chalk used to write on the slate board. Once a month, it was the duty of selected students to wash the blackboard. This required careful attention to the amount of water used. Too much and the chalk powder would become a sticky mess on the floor, and if the boards were not dried properly the chalk turned into a paste when you tried to write on the board — it was very difficult to clean the board once the wet chalk dried. While one group of students were washing the black-boards (actually slate-boards), another group would be assigned the task of cleaning the felt blackboard erasers. After much erasing, the felt erasers would become coated with white chalk dust. Students would take the erasers outside and slapped them together, creating a great cloud of white dust that covered the face, arms, and hair of those cleaning the erasers. Each week, the students were responsible for sweeping the floors. Yes, there was no janitorial service. This sweeping was usually divided between boys and girls. One week, the girls swept, and the next week, the boys swept. To keep the dust down, the county provided a red, granular, oily, substance that we put on the floor by scattering fistfuls of the chemical substance and then swept the oily, granular chemicals and floor dirt into the dust pans. I have often wondered what cancer-causing chemicals we were using to "keep the dust down"!

Although the school facilities were primitive by "modern" standards, it still provided an excellent educational foundation for those of us lucky enough to have experienced it. At the beginning of our 5th grade, (1957), Rockport and most rural Mississippi schools were closed, and students were consolidated into larger schools. The Rockport students went to the elementary school in Wesson. High School age students went to the High School on the campus of Copiah-Lincoln Junior College, also in Wesson. Wesson was approximately 20 miles from our home.

During our entire school experience from Rockport to Wesson, grades 1 through 12, there was only one fight which required a teacher to intervene in order to stop the fight. In those days, when teachers were asked to list problems caused by students, teachers would generally list things like "talking out of turn," "chewing gum in class," or "running in the halls." There were no armed guards, no locked doors, or required check-in/sign-in when an adult visited the school. Donald and I have often noted that we never saw or heard of an instance of "bullying." But in our modern, progressive, politically correct, secular humanist era, things have changed — and no one seems to care about the "why" it has changed.

Strong Hope Elementary School circa 1950. (MDAH)

Georgetown High School circa 1950. (Photo MDAH)

Chapter 4:

BREAKFAST IN THE RURAL SOUTH

WHAT DID YOU HAVE for breakfast this morning? Did you eat it with the entire family? Did you say grace before eating? In our modern rush, rush society breakfast often consists of grabbing a muffin, piece of toast, or a bagel on the way out the door. Rush, rush, rush, hurry, hurry, hurry, seems to be the mantra of our "modern" society. As *Uncle Seth* said in one of his stories, "They are rushing to their graves, rushing to their graves." Things were different *back in the day*.

We generally got up at sun rise, no alarm clock needed because it was vocally announced by the old, red rooster on top of the chicken house. In addition, every other rooster in the surrounding farms were doing their best to outdo our rooster's crowing. Mom would already be up and getting breakfast ready. If we had farm work to do, Dad would be out at the barn giving the mule his breakfast; putting the harness on the mule; and selecting the correct plow for the day's work. If Dad had a painting or carpenter job to do, he would be loading his pick-up truck. During the school year, Donald and I would get dressed for school and do the usual last-minute work on our homework or cramming for a test—all of which we should have done the prior afternoon instead of playing outside until well after sundown! The school bus arrived at our house around 6:45 each school morning. We always wore clean clothes each day. Mom took great pride in the fact that "You may not have the best clothes, but you will have clean clothes when you leave for school." Of course, after a day of enjoying recess, they were never clean when we returned home after school. During the summer, we would put on our work clothes and go outside to help Dad. Our work clothes consisted of blue jeans, a white tee shirt, and tennis shoes. The cost of blue jeans in 1960 was between $2.98 to $3.16 plus tax, and the cost of tennis shoes in 1960 was between $2.00 and $5.00. Mom never bought the more expensive blue jeans brand such as Levi but opted for the less expensive brand Tuff Nut—made in Little Rock, Arkansas.

When we had farm work to do, breakfast consisted of homemade biscuits, homemade butter, cane syrup called molasses when we had it, or Blackburn syrup, which was the cheapest brand of store bought syrup Mom could find, thick cut bacon, brown gravy, occasionally grits, milk for the boys, and coffee for Mom and Dad. The entire family gathered around the table, Dad would say grace, or sometimes Mom would ask one of us boys to say grace, and then we would eat and talk about the plans for the day. We did not realize it, but eating together is an important social event that helps to knit the family together.

All societies use feasts days and other social gatherings centered around food as a way to celebrate special occasions while enjoying each other's company. Such gatherings also serve the important social purpose of binding community ties between people who share a common inheritance of culture, language, and faith. It is a way of socially reconfirming peoples' mutual relationships as a community composed of folks who share a common culture—which is the opposite of politically correct, cultural diversity. It is a way of strengthening the ties of *kith and kin*. In the 1950s churches would have what we used to call "dinner on the ground." *Back in the day*, on the appointed Sunday, each family would bring a dish of food, meat, bread, or sweet tea, and set it out on tables constructed under oak trees. After church services were over all would share and enjoy the meal. Today, it is more commonly called a "pot luck supper," which is served in the church's air-conditioned family life center. It's not the same as eating *dinner* (noon meal) outside, but it serves the same purpose plus the added comfort of modern air-conditioning—which we all have grown so used to that we now consider it a necessity of life. Donald and I have often joked that we could get rid of all the Yankees in the South if we could just turn off all the air-conditioners. The only problem is that we would lose about 90% of our fellow Southerners as well!

One of my favorite photographs of sharecroppers is the one of the Lonnie Fair family saying grace before they eat their *supper*. Black or white, we all shared a common religious faith and an understanding of our utter dependence on God's blessing to get through this life and into the next. We all had a firm faith that a better life would be obtained through faith in Christ Jesus. The religious faith of most Southerners was, and hopefully still is, that we have awaiting us a "Crown in Glory" for those who truly believe.

On school mornings, Mom would usually have hot oatmeal and chocolate milk waiting for us. The chocolate milk was a special treat. It was made with the dark, bitter, Hersey's baking chocolate powder.

Breakfast in the Rural South

She bought it instead of the sweet easy to mix chocolate power because it was less expensive, it lasted longer, and she could use it for baking cakes. Extravagance was unknown in those days; we wasted nothing, and we lived by the economic creed that "a penny saved is a penny earned." We were lucky—unlike many Southerners in the prior generation—we never suffered from hunger. More about hunger in the chapter 19, "Starvation—the Hungry South."

The Lonnie Fair family saying grace. (Photo LOC).

Chapter 5:

AFTER-SCHOOL SNACKS

WHEN BOYS AND GIRLS get home after attending school all day, one of the first things they do is to head to the kitchen and grab a quick snack. It was no different for the Kennedy Twins. It took the school bus around 45 minutes to an hour to get us home after school. There were no "store bought" snacks waiting for us at home. Our after-school snacks usually consisted of cold corn bread eaten as we went outside to do our chores. Sometimes, on cold, winter days, Mom would have baked sweet potatoes waiting for us or a fried fruit-turnover. Apple or peach were the main fruits used for the turnovers. Now and then, our Great Aunt Vivian (Eleanor Vivian Little Kennedy, 1880-1962) would send over some of her Tea Cakes, "for the boys." After the family obtained a small freezer (we always called it the "deep freezer"), Mom occasionally used some of the blackberries we had gathered and frozen the prior summer to make blackberry cobbler. These treats were rare, but that seemed to make them that much more special.

Dixieland Cola.
(Photo MS AG Museum).

Today when I stop at a service station to fill the car with gas, I think nothing of going inside and purchasing a *Coke* or a candy bar. But when we were growing-up, Mom and Dad could not afford to casually spend money even on small things like a *Coke*. Mom would occasionally purchase a carton of six RC (Royal Crown) Colas. She would carefully ration the drinks to make sure they lasted a long time. Since there were two of us, she would not give each of us a bottle of RC Cola. She would take a cold RC out of the refrigerator, open it, and pour half into a glass. Donald and I would take turns—one would get to drink from the RC bottle, and the other from the glass. We always remembered whose turn it was to get the RC bottle and who had to drink from the glass. Drinking from the RC bottle seemed, at the time, to be a real treat as opposed to drinking the RC Cola out of a glass.

It was not until we were 12 or 13 that Mom purchased "store bought" glasses for the *dinner* table. Until then, the *dinner* table glassware was a collection of glasses from store bought jelly or jam containers. At that time, many jelly and jam producers packaged their products in nice looking glasses as an inducement for the poor classes to purchase their product. This marketing technique was very common in the South and perhaps in other areas where the purchasing public consisted of folks with limited income. I recall seeing some of the poorer, older women in the community wearing dresses made from feed sacks. Livestock feed was sold in 100-pound sacks. Many feed providers used a cheap, nicely died, cotton sack that had a print of small flowers on the sack. The poorer women saved the sacks and used them as material for making dresses. Women wearing homemade dresses from feed sack material was, at one time, very common in the rural South. By the mid-1950s in our part of the rural South, it was becoming less common to see poor women wearing sackcloth dresses. A century after *the War*, things were beginning to improve economically for the poor whites and blacks in the South. (When I refer to "Southerners," I include all Southerners, both black and white).

After eating our snack, we headed outside to take care of our chores. The two of us could complete our chores in a relatively short time. The chores consisted of calling up the cows (bringing them from the front pasture to the stomp lot at the barn), slopping the hogs, feeding the chickens, milking the cow, and during the winter months, bringing in the *"fat lighter"* kindling wood and *toting* oak firewood for the fireplace, and stacking it on the back porch. Up until we were around 4 or 5-years old mom cooked with a wood burning stove. The wood burning stove had a metal (tin) chimney that went up through the ceiling, through the attic and out the roof of the house. The metal chimney had a concrete housing set in the ceiling and the roof to prevent the hot, tin chimney from igniting the wooden ceiling or roof and setting the house on fire. Mom was kept busy cooking and trying to keep two toddlers away for the hot stove. We learned early the meaning of the phrase *Once burned, twice warned.*

After the chores were done, we had the choice of staying outside and playing or going inside and spending time on our studies.

Unfortunately, outside usually won out! Being less than diligent students was a poor choice, but it seemed OK at the time. A word of warning for all young people. There is an old Jewish curse that says, "May the indiscretions of your youth become the infirmities of your old age." May the youth of today take the advice of those who have learned from the school of hard knocks. Or, as I often have said, "I have wisdom born of sad experience." Parents try to advise their teenage children because we do not want them to spend too much time in the school of hard knocks. We have been there and done that!

Wood burning stove similar to the one Mom cooked with when Donald and I were 4 or 5 years old. (Photo from MS AG Museum Jackson, MS).

Chapter 6:

TAKING GUNS TO SCHOOL

HUNTING, FISHING, CAMPING, and especially guns were a major part of life for boys growing up in *Dixie* when Donald and I were young. Donald and I got our first BB gun when we were nine years old — and no, we did not shoot our eyes out! It was the only Christmas present we got that year, but it was great! We each had our own Daisy BB gun. Of course, it came with the usual caution to treat it like any other gun — don't point it at anyone, always assume it is loaded, and make sure you identify your target before you squeeze the trigger. We would save every penny that came our way to purchase more ammunition (nickel packets of BBs). Later, as we got to be teenagers, we obtained a shotgun and a .22 caliber rifle. The handling of shotguns and rifles came naturally. Guns and hunting have always been a natural part of living in the South.

RC Cola bottle, coal oil, & green pine needles.

Note gun in back window.
(Photo U. S. National Archives)

This natural ability with firearms has been acknowledged by Yankee gun experts. During the War for Southern Independence, Confederate soldiers hit their targets at a rate of two or three to one when compared to Yankee soldiers. Unfortunately, Yankees outnumbered us three or four to one! The better marksmanship of Southern soldiers was the result of our rural environment. Most Confederate soldiers came from rural areas that were still heavily wooded. They spent a great deal of time camping, hunting, and fishing. Most Yankee soldiers came from cities or well-developed rural areas where one farm ended, and another began—where there were less wooded areas and forests. Toward the last years of *the War*, a very large percentage of Yankee soldiers came from Irish immigrants (basically mercenaries) who were fleeing starvation in Ireland. The English Empire that then occupied Ireland made sure the Irish did not have easy access to firearms. Empires don't want their subjects to have the ability to defend themselves. Most of the Irish troops that came into the Yankee army did not have a lot of experience handling firearms. But there were many Yanks who were good with firearms, although not as good as we were. I have read accounts from Confederate soldiers who were very impressed with Yankee troops from western states, such as Iowa—states where the young men spent a lot of time on horseback, hunting, and other outdoor activities. Shortly after *the War*, a Yankee officer established the National Rifle Association (NRA) because he was concerned about the poor marksmanship of his Yankee troops during *the War*. One of my nephews told me about his first days at boot camp—where young recruits are trained to be soldiers. He said that there were young men there who grew up in cities and who had never even held a rifle!

On Friday mornings during the fall, it was not uncommon to see teenage boys bringing their guns to school. When Donald and I wanted to go hunting over the weekend with our friends who lived near Wesson, we would take our guns and put them on the bus behind the bus driver—always with his permission obtained as we were getting on the bus. When we reached the school, we would take the guns to the principal's office. He would look up, smile, and ask "*Yawl going hunting this weekend?*" And then without waiting for a reply, he would instruct us, "Just put them over there in the corner." At the end of the day, we would go to the principal's office and retrieve our guns, meet our friends and ride home with them on their school bus.

Boys driving their pick-up trucks to school had their guns hanging on a gun rack behind the truck's bench seat fully visible through the truck's back window. In all of the twelve years of our school experience, we never had the slightest hint of gun violence, even though guns were readily available. I can recall only one fist-fight during the same time period. What has changed? Have we as a society become more "progressive" in worldly things at the expense of those spiritual values that are necessary to maintain a moral and civil society?

Guns in the hands of moral people represent no danger to peaceful, law-abiding people. We learned this from male teachers in elementary school. Men who had served in the U.S. military during World War II. Brother Douglas, the minister of our local Baptist church, was also one of our elementary school teachers. He served in the Army Air Corps (this was when the Air Force was a part of the Army). He regaled us with stories about his experiences learning to shoot military rifles and how he had to parachute out of his transport plane when it was hit by German anti-aircraft fire. He was part of the generation that fought the great patriotic war against Nazism. Like men have been doing for thousands of years, he answered his country's call and put his life at risk to protect his family back home. When modern day radical leftwing feminists make claims about male privilege, they never factor in the millions of men who have died in innumerable wars defending the women and children back home.

Brother Douglas in military uniform circa 1941.

When Rebel Was Cool

Arkansas boys with gun circa 1935 (LOC).

Guns and patriotism have always come naturally to Southerners. (A word of caution: There is a major difference between patriotism and nationalism). Brother Douglas was a true patriot. He told the class about how important it was to respect the country's flag. He instructed us that it was a sign of disrespect to allow the flag to touch the ground. Years later, as a *Civil War* re-enactor, I learned the origin of that tradition. Before the days of radio communications, the primary way a commander could tell a company of troops where to position themselves on the battle line was to command the flag bearer to move (post) to a given place on the battlefield, and the company would "form up on the flag." The company flag was unique to each company. When your company moved forward, you would always keep the flag in sight. If the flag goes down, the company loses its unit cohesion and becomes vulnerable to being overrun by the enemy. It was considered the highest honor to be the flag bearer, but it was also the point of greatest danger—the enemy would try to shoot the flag bearer in an effort to disorganize their opponent. Today, when we protect the flag from touching the ground, we not only honor the flag, but we also honor those brave men who offered their lives while serving as their unit's flag bearer and all who fought under that flag.

Brother Douglas was very concerned about the worldwide advancement of atheistic communism. He saw in communism an evil and dangerous ideology even greater than that of Nazism. This was during the height of the Cold War. Everyone expected the Russians would attack us eventually. In the 1950s, the United States Air Force even re-organized a civilian sky watch organization—the Ground Observer Corps originally organized during World War II. The purpose for the Ground Observers was to help detect Russian planes that might try to sneak into our air space with the intent of dropping nuclear bombs. One of the radio ads used by the U.S. Air Force to encourage civilian involvement declared: "It may not be a very cheerful thought, but the Reds [Russians] right now have about a thousand bombers quite capable of destroying 89 cities in one raid.... Won't you help protect your country, your town, your children?"

Taking Guns to School

Mom and Dad's certificates as part of the Cold War Ground Observer Corps

Hundreds of thousands of patriotic Americans joined the Observer Corps. Brother Douglas made sure that our community joined and did our part to keep the Russians at bay.

I recall, in the late 1950s, one of my female cousins told me about a terrible dream she had the previous night. She dreamed that the Russians had parachuted troops into our community, and we had to fight them! Even children were frightened by the specter of a Russian invasion or nuclear attack. It is hard for people today to understand the anxiety that permeated American society during the Cold War. A large part of this fear was generated by the military that claimed there was a bomber gap between the Russians and the United States — the claim was that the Russian communists had more attack aircraft than we did. Therefore, according to the military "experts" and their allies in Congress, we needed to build more planes and other military equipment. This intentionally created national anxiety was a great windfall to what President Eisenhower called the "military industrial complex." About a decade later, the same folks claimed that there was now a missile gap. It was another boon for the military industrial complex. At the end of the Cold War, we found out that these so called "gaps" never existed! But fear of communism was used by those in power to enrich businessmen and politicians with close connections to the military industrial complex. But the taxes used to enrich the military industrial complex were extracted from America's middle class. We should always remember the warning that James Madison, a founding father from Virginia, left for us, "Where there is power, and will to use it, wrong will be done." Never trust politicians to always "do the right thing!"

This was hung in the living room of the Kennedy Twins' home. Mom and Dad did their best to live by it.
It proffers the following advice:
In such an hour ye thinketh not, the Son of Man cometh. Rules for today: Do the things you would like to be doing; Go to places you would like to be found; Say the thing you would like to be saying: When Jesus Comes.

Chapter 7:

OUR CHORES: WORKING THE FARM

WHILE WE WERE GROWING up in the rural South, there were two classes of people. There were poor, white Southerners, and there were poor, black Southerners. As a general rule, rural, white Southerners were not as poor as rural, black Southerners, but there were always exceptions to this general rule. Regardless of color, all knew that to *keep soul and body together* (to stay alive), each member of the family had to carry his or her share of the load. Typical chores for us when we were eight or nine years old included such tasks as bringing in firewood during the winter months. There was a large wood pile in the backyard. Our task, during the winter months, was to bring in enough firewood for that evening and the next day. We would stack the firewood on the back porch. Every evening during the year, our job was to call the cows in from the front pasture (land we owned across the road from the house and barn), open the gates to the barn (the stomp lot) and move them across

Butter mold and hand cranked churn for making butter. From Kennedy family collection.

the road. We fed the cows a small amount of corn each afternoon shortly before sundown. The cows knew this, so they responded to our call—we didn't need to go looking for them or round them up. Our "herd" of cattle was between 6 to 8 cows and calves. Other tasks included feeding the chickens and slopping the hogs (feeding the hogs). The final task of the evening was to milk the cow. We milked the cow in the same barn our Grandfather Kennedy built circa 1900. The old barn originally had a white oak shingle roof which was replaced with tin in the 1940s. We tore it down and built another barn in the early 1960s. The old barn's tin roof was reused on the new barn. The old tin was still in use as late as 2010!

Milking a cow is one of many farm skills our father taught us. Rural folks in the South at that time did not have a lot of disposable income. We grew most of our food. Every family that owned their farm had a "milk cow." The correct term is *milch cow*, but most folks use the incorrect term "milk cow." The milk cow provided the family with not only "fresh" milk, but also cream—which would be collected, turned (churned) into butter, and formed into a block with a butter mold. After churning the cream into butter, the "butter milk" would be poured off and saved. Butter milk would be used for baking biscuits and corn bread. The old folks distinguished butter milk from fresh milk by calling fresh milk *sweet milk*.

To collect the cream, the *sweet milk* would be poured into large ceramic pots, covered with a clean cloth (to prevent insects from getting into the cream) and allowed to stand overnight during which time the "cream would rise to the top." The next day mom collected the cream, which had rose (had risen) to the top. Overnight, the sweet milk would turn to clabber. Clabber is a term that is all but lost in modern times. It is the curdled, thickened, and sour substance that raw (unpasteurized) sweet milk turns into if it is not refrigerated. Prior to refrigeration Southerners would keep a bowl of clabber handy, mix it with cool well water and serve it at breakfast if sweet milk was not available. Mom told us that when she was growing-up, they would take a small bit of clabber and put it on a spoon behind bitter medicine to make it easier to swallow the medicine. In our day, at our home, we added the clabber to the hog slop and feed it to the hogs.

Notice I said, "Every family that owned land had a milk cow." Not every rural Southern family owned land. Sharecroppers were landless poor—some scholars classified them as landless peasants. The numbers of sharecroppers had decreased by the 1950s. Thankfully, by the mid-1960s, the Southern economy and farm mechanization had improved to the point that the system of sharecropping died out. At its height, there were over 8.5 million sharecroppers in the South—slightly over 60% were white Southerners. In a 1940s speech, Mississippi

Our Chores

Southern child picking cotton circa 1940. (LOC).

Senator James Eastland described the dreadful system of sharecropping as a form of slavery! Yet, the Federal government did little, if anything, to alleviate the suffering down South. Donald and I detail this in "Punished With Poverty-the Suffering South."

At nine years of age, Donald and I were expected to be able to hoe out the garden during the spring and most of the summer. Summer time meant that we were free from school work, but Mom and Dad made sure that we had plenty to keep us busy. Mom was fond of saying, "Idle hands is the Devil's workshop." We learned the difference between hoeing cotton and chopping cotton — hoeing is the process by which the hoe is used to remove weeds, and chopping is when the hoe is used to thin out the cotton plants. Cotton needs plenty of room to grow and plenty of sunshine to mature, so the rows are spaced wider than with other crops, and once the plants begin to grow, they are manually thinned out with the hoe. Thankfully, Dad decided early on that he would use his skills as a carpenter and painter to *make a living* as opposed to relying strictly on farming. But there was still plenty of farm chores on our forty-five-*acre* farm to keep us busy.

By the time we were teenagers, we were expected to do the plowing while dad was at work — as a carpenter, painter, or welder. By that time, we no longer planted cotton, but there were still several *acres* of corn that had to be plowed. By late fall, we would begin to gather the dried corn. Farm grown corn was used for corn meal, chicken feed, and cattle feed. During the week, while dad was at work, Donald and I would pull the mature corn off the dried corn stalk, and place it on the ground in *heap* rows — which was actually a pile ever 20 to 30 feet, consisting of the corn we pulled from corn stalks on three adjacent rows. Harvesting corn by hand is referred to as "pulling corn." Cotton harvested by hand is referred to as "picking cotton." While pulling corn, dried field peas would also be gathered. We planted field peas when we planted the corn. Each row of corn would have one or two hills of peas. During early summer, we "picked peas" while the plants were still green, and Mom would cook them for *supper*. By late summer we would gather the dried field peas to be stored for that Southern delicacy "black eye peas." I have often reminded my children that General Lee claimed that black eye peas were the only friend the Southern soldier could always count on.

Harvesting Irish potatoes is done in the late summer or early fall. It is referred to as "digging potatoes" because the edible part of the potato grows in the ground and must be dug-up. Dad hitched the mule to a turning plow, set the plow point deep, and rolled the soil over, exposing the potatoes. He then hitched the mule to a ground slide. We then gathered the potatoes and place them in the ground slide. Dad then drove the mule and slide to the barn. We had a dedicated area in the corn crib where we unloaded and stored our potatoes. The potatoes kept (remained edible while stored) just fine during the fall, winter, and through spring. The heat of mid to late summer would tend to cause the potatoes to begin to rot, but by then a new crop was ready, or just about ready, to begin using. Collecting new, small potatoes to cook the same day is referred to as "grubbing potatoes." This is done prior to the potato plants maturing and when the potatoes in the barn have "gone bad."

Peanuts were another crop that could be grown, but we usually swapped out with the neighbor for his peanuts. Peanuts are also a crop that grows in the ground (the edible portion is beneath the surface of the ground). The process of harvesting peanuts is similar to digging potatoes — and harvesting peanuts is referred to as digging peanuts — but each peanut must be pulled off the plant roots. With potatoes, you can simply pick the potatoes up off the turned-up soil with minimal effort to remove the tuber (potato) from the plant roots. But with peanuts, you must shake off the soil and pull each peanut shell off the vine (actually the root although we always called it picking the peanuts off the vine).

Dad *gave up on* growing cotton as a cash crop when Donald and I were around ten years old. Growing a few *acres* of cotton was one of the primary ways most farmers who owned less than a hundred acres earned spending money. The Kennedy Twins have hoed, chopped, and picked cotton, but we were not disappointed when the last cotton on our place was sent to the cotton gin and sold. When the family needed a little extra cash — over and above what Dad made as a carpenter — we would take a young steer to market or cut a load of pulpwood and take it to the local general store. Local general stores located next to the GM&O railroad purchased the pulpwood. Each general store had a dedicated railroad car on a side track. The store owner purchased pulpwood from the locals. We loaded our pulpwood onto the railroad car. When the railroad car was full, the general store manager sold the wood to the pulpwood mill, and a freight train hooked up and took the

Our Chores

Donnie Kennedy and Bill Littleton demonstrating use of cross cut saw – Point, LA.

wood to the paper mill— the mill would turn the pulpwood into various forms of paper.

Cutting pulpwood is an arduous task. You must select large pine trees but not ones that are large enough to eventually use as logs and not so small that the mill will not accept the cut wood. Back in the day, we did not have power tools such as chainsaws. The tree had to be cut down using a manual two handled saw called a "cross-cut saw." It required two strong men to pull the saw. Dad would take one end and, Donald and I would take turns pulling the other end. After the tree was felled, we used our axes to remove the limbs from the tree trunk. Dad would mark it at approximately five-foot intervals. We then used the cross-cut saw to cut the tree trunk into five-foot sections of pulp wood. After cutting enough to make a truck load, we then loaded the wood onto the truck, and off we would go to the pulpwood lot (the general store's area for loading the pulpwood onto the general store's assigned railroad car).

Pulpwood is primarily cut from pine trees. The lower South contains pine trees stretching from North and South Carolina, Georgia, and north Florida all the way across to east Texas. It is referred to by foresters as the great pine belt. The sap of the pine tree is rich in a sticky substance called resin—although we always called it *rosin*. Compared to the sap of other trees, pine sap is very sticky and flammable. The flammability of the pine sap posed no problem when cutting "cord wood" (another term for pulpwood), but its stickiness is a major problem when trying to pull-push a cross-cut saw through the wood. The "pull" stroke is the cutting stroke, while the "push" stroke is to make sure the saw does not drag as it slides away from the person not pulling. But if you "push" too much, it will cause the saw blade to buckle, which will destroy the smooth back and forth sawing rhythm. Folks cutting pulpwood solved the sticky pine sap problem by putting *coal oil* in a soft drink bottle (we refused to use anything other than a Royal Crown Cola or RC Cola bottle) and stuff the bottle's open end with pine needles. We used this to occasionally brush the cross-cut saw blade with coal oil. The *coal oil* would break down the pine sap (resin), which allowed the blade to slide back and forth without "gumming up" or freezing in the tree trunk. This technique was also used when cutting down sweet gum trees.

Modern folks tend to think of rural Southerners as being less learned or intelligent than those who dwell in big cities. The rural South, *back in the day* and even today, has a per capita income lower than the national average. Learning to survive in an impoverished area of the country required a great deal of individual competence. For example; it required a considerable amount of skill to learn the push-pull rhythm required to use the cross-cut saw. It also requires a considerable skill to know how to sharpen the cutting teeth of a cross-cut saw, not to mention being knowledgeable enough about forestry to select the correct trees to cut, how to safely cut them down, and understanding enough about the market price of cord wood to know the best time to take a load of pulpwood to market.

Mom's youngest brother
Bidwell Adam Berry circa 1950

Dad provided the family's income by working locally as a carpenter and painter. One year he actually earned a little over $10,000. He was really proud of that year's work. Due to government created inflation, that does not seem to be much money. But, $10,000 in 1960 would be equal to around $80,000 in today's (2019) dollars. That means that it would take $80,000 today to purchase the same items as could have been purchased with $10,000 in 1960. The median household income for Mississippi in 2016 was around $42,000, while the median household income for the entire United States was around $58,000. Inflation is a way for politicians in the Federal government to tax the people without having to put their political decisions to a public vote in Congress! The impact of government caused inflation always falls hardest on the poor. Politicians like to call it inflation because it causes the general public to focus on increasing prices that stores charge. In reality, it is not increasing prices but decreasing value of government money. The decreasing value of government money is caused by politicians, not the free market. But so much for economics—let's get back to the "good-ole-days."

During the spring and summer, various vegetables, fruits, and berries ripened. The fruit had to be gathered and processed within a very short window of time. We had a peach tree that grew next to the chicken house. It would always produce wonderful peaches. I am sure that being next to the chicken house had a lot to do with the tree's productivity. Chicken dropping is very rich in nitrogen and has been used as a natural fertilizer since ancient days—in today's world, we would call it an "organic" fertilizer.

Once the peaches ripened, we had only a week or so to gather them, process them by removing the large peach seed in the middle, cut them up, and put them in canning jars. After Mom and Dad purchased a small freezer, we put the cut peaches in freezing bags. Blackberries grew wild. We carefully noted where each briar patch was by the white blooms the briars put on in the early spring. Each bloom produced a small berry bud which grew and turned from green in early spring, to bright red a few weeks later, and then to a dark black around the end of May or early June. We made picking blackberries a family affair. There were many blackberry briar-patches on our land. Rabbits and small rodents like to use them as a place to hide from dogs, foxes, and bobcats. (Have you watched the story of Brer Rabbit in Walt Disney's "Song of the South?" It is a folktale that was brought to the South by African slaves. The Southern Native Americans, Cherokees, also had a very similar folktale). The briar patch proved no hindrance to snakes. Snakes would often enter the briar patch to hunt rabbits and rodents. Rattlesnakes seemed to prefer briar patches. You

Mom's oldest brother James Walter Berry circa 1944

have to be very careful when picking blackberries, to make sure you didn't step on a snake or get snake bit when reaching for berries hanging close to the ground. After we collected several gallon molasses buckets of blackberries, Mom would then process them into jams and jellies. In addition to jams and jellies, Mom would make blackberry cobbler. This was always a favorite treat for this time of the year. Occasionally, Dad would bring home ice from the ice house in town, and we would enjoy homemade ice cream with peach or blackberry cobbler. Blackberry-picking time was a time of great family fun—time spent outside with Mom.

Aunt Vivian told us that her father said that the boys coming home from *the War* had to walk home with very little or no provisions. She said that the discharged soldiers would often spend their mornings picking blackberries because many mornings, that was the only thing they could find to eat in the war-ravaged South. *The War* ended in April and May of 1865. Many of the discharged Confederate soldiers had to walk most of the way home. By the time some of the discharged soldiers got back from places like Virginia and Georgia, it would have put them back in Mississippi just as the blackberries were turning black. Stories like this from our Great Aunt is how Southerners of our day learned their history. To us, it was not history—it was family. I never questioned her, just always assumed it was true. Years later, while doing research, I read an account written by one of our Southern soldiers—who eventually became the Chair of Mathematics at Louisiana State University in Baton Rouge—who walked home from North Carolina to Louisiana after the end of *the War*. He stated that at times, ripening blackberries was all they could find to eat. Family history verified!

Chapter 8:

WHICH IS BETTER: MAN'S WEALTH OR GOD'S WEALTH

AUNT MINNIE BELL KENNEDY LONGLEY (1896-1991) was the oldest of the eight children born to Grand Mother and Grand Father Kennedy. Dad (Burnice Edgar Kennedy 1909-1988) was the youngest. Two of the eight did not survive. Dad's twin sister (Bernice 1909), died shortly after birth, and a brother, Luie Virgil (1899-1904), died as a young boy. He fell while getting out of the family's carriage. Dad said that they thought that when he fell, he hit his stomach on the carriage's metal foot step. From the description of the accident, he most likely ruptured his spleen and died several days later from internal hemorrhaging. Dad's twin sister, Bernice, was buried in a homemade coffin. Granddaddy Kennedy made the coffin out of a hollow oak tree. He cut the tree down, cut a three-foot section out of the log, split it in two, smoothed out the inside, and covered the inside with a coarse cotton blanket. The final resting place of Dad's twin sister and Virgil's earthly remains are now known only to God. Such was the hard life in the turn of the century (early 1900s) rural South. It would not be until the early 1950s before a hospital was built at the county seat, Hazlehurst, Mississippi. A trip to Hazlehurst in the early 1950s required at least 45 minutes to an hour traveling over dusty (during the summer) or muddy (during the winter) gravel roads to get there and then the same time to return.

Luie Virgil Kennedy (1899-1904)

When Rebel Was Cool

Bosses of the Senate, during the post-War Gilded Age. Rich Yankees control the government — poor Southerners endure and pay for the government. (Photo Wikipedia Commons).

During America's post-War "Gilded Age" (1870 to 1900), while the financial and commercial elites on Wall Street and the rest of America were enjoying economic expansion, the rural South was still mired in dust, mud, and enduring material poverty. The same was true, but to a lesser degree, during America's tremendous economic expansion post-World War II (1946-1965). That is not to say that there was not poverty outside of the South, but the poverty the South suffered under touched a much larger proportion of the South's population than did poverty in states outside of the South. This generalized, South-wide poverty was intentionally and or callously imposed upon both black and white Southerners by the victors in *the War*. The fact that the South's poverty was intentionally inflicted upon us by the victors in the War for Southern Independence made the sufferings of Southern poverty even worse, at least from a psychological perspective. Southerners were forced to watch as the North became rich and prosperous while the South languished in poverty — an unnatural poverty forced upon them by the victorious North. *Vae Victus*, or woe to the vanquished — the motto of empires.

Which Is Better

In an almost unbelievably frank and honest editorial in the "U.S. News and World Report," April 17, 1961, the Northern editor contrasted the way in which the victorious United States treated the defeated Germans and Japanese after World War II with the calloused indifference and deplorable poverty inflicted upon the people of the South after the Yankee victory in the so-called *Civil War*. Within five years after Germany and Japan surrendered, these defeated nations' economies had mostly recovered and were expanding. This was not the case for the post-War South—even 50 years after our forced surrender! The people of the South were forced to *make-do* with the little remaining resources they had available. The greatest resource we had was something no earthly enemy could take away—our inheritance of traditional, Bible-based, values.

Southern society's traditional attitude toward material prosperity helped post War Southerners to endure. Material wealth is important to any society, but, by traditional Southern thinking, the measurement of social value is more than a simple accounting of material values. A society's worth cannot be measured and totaled on an accountant's spreadsheet or the valuations on Wall Street's ticker tapes (stock prices). This spiritual interpretation of our society helped to sustain post-War Southerners as well as successive Southern generations. Perhaps because the South suffered invasion, conquest, and occupation, this first-hand experience helped Southerners to understand that worldly success is not a proper measurement or criteria for morality, worth, or social value. It allowed an entire people to look beyond their material inadequacies relative to the rest of the country— remember the post-War South was and is still the poorest section/region of the United States. The ability of post-War Southerners to look beyond the intentional impoverishment imposed upon them by the Yankee victors prevented the

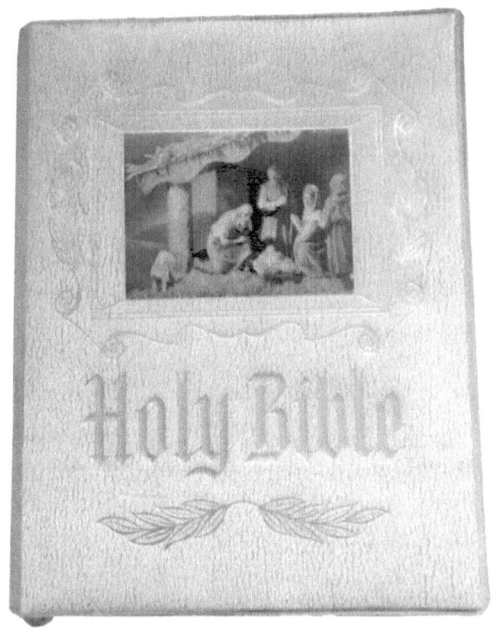

Mom and Dad's Family Bible. Purchased in 1988 for $47.98.

development of mass anger and resentment toward the nation—the United States of America—from which the people of the South had received so much heartache, abuse, death, destruction, and intentional impoverishment.

Post-War Southerners became the most patriotic of all Americans, as indicated by the proportion of Southern men serving in the U.S. military. Former Confederate General Wheeler and other former Confederates served in the U.S. Army during the Spanish American War (1898); the most decorated soldier in World War I was Alvin York of Tennessee; and, in World War II, Audie Murphy from Texas was one of the most highly decorated soldiers in that war. Patriotism and a sense of military valor gave Southerners a reason to cling to the memory of the glories and gallantry of their Confederate ancestors. From the Spanish American War through the Vietnam War (1898 to 1975), the South's effusion of blood in the U.S. military purchased the nation's respect for the military traditions of the Confederacy. There was a time when the United States Post Office issued commendatory stamps honoring Confederate Generals; the U.S. Mint struck coins honoring the Confederacy; and the U.S. Navy even had submarines named for Confederate Generals Robert E. Lee and Stonewall Jackson. But those days are gone in today's secular humanist, left of center, politically correct, America. More recently, the ruling elites in America's political, educational, and entertainment establishments have rejected the South's contribution to the nation's defense. The nation's elites no longer see any value in the South's patriotic devotion to the nation that invaded, conquered, occupied, and exploited us.

When a people's future is encumbered, limited, and exploited by overwhelming outside forces, then it is only natural for the people to look to the past for inspiration, while clinging to the hope of better days to come. Shortly before Donald and I left home to begin our study as Respiratory Therapists, the family received a copy of a letter outlining the family's history. This short letter demonstrated the resilience of our people, even when faced with poverty.

Aunt Minnie Bell Kennedy Longley, Dad's oldest sister, sent a letter describing the struggles her mother and father went through just to survive in the rural South. In her short letter, she described how her father, my Grandfather Theodore Prentis Kennedy (1869-1931), had to work as an indentured servant for seven years to earn the right to forty *acres* of virgin forest and bottom land. He and Grandmother Hettie L. Hamilton Kennedy (1871-1935) were engaged the entire seven years. When his indentureship was complete, all he had was one old mule, forty acres of virgin land, a few plows, hand tools, and a new bride. He and Grandmother married and set-up their home place—which was

Which Is Better

only a few yards from the home that Dad would build in 1946 and in which the Kennedy Twins would be born a year later.

Aunt Minnie Bell described the newlyweds' first house. It was a log house, the same one in which she was born. It had a dirt floor. There was no glass in the windows. Her crib was handmade by Granddaddy Kennedy out of small oak branches and white oak strips—the same type of wood strips they would use to make cotton baskets. Their *dinner* table was made of split oak logs. Granddaddy Kennedy had to clear all the virgin land by hand before he could begin tilling the land and planting his crops. Small tree stumps had to be dug around and pulled out while the larger ones were left standing and simply plowed around for years until they rotted. Softwood trees, such as Sweet Gum, would usually rot away in a couple of years. Hardwood trees, such as oaks, took several more years, depending on the size of the stump. But the longleaf pine stumps were so full of *rosin*, that it took decades for them to rot away. Some of them were still in place when Donald and I were young boys in the late-1950s.

The photo of Dad and Uncle Ellis T. Kennedy (1906-1994) holding the fish they caught while fishing in the Pearl River tells more about the poverty and the determination of our people than mere words could ever tell. Notice the ragged condition of their clothes and their bare feet. That photo was taken circa 1919. When that photograph was taken more than half a century had passed since the end of the so-called *Civil War*. Yet, poverty was still the greater part of the South's inheritance within Lincoln's supreme Federal Union. It was a Union in which the South was compelled, at the point of bloody bayonets, to remain. The South became an impoverished captive nation within a rich and powerful nation. After *the War*, the United States became a rich, globalist empire. Lincoln's new Union was one to which impoverished Southerners were forced to pay tribute in the form of taxes and tariffs. So much for the "consent of the governed," as proclaimed in the 1776 Declaration of Independence. That old, faded, black and white

Dad and Uncle Ellis circa 1919.

photograph of my Dad and his brother from a simple rural family's photo album tells more about the South's true history than anything a Yankee educated "intellectual" will ever know or understand. Even if the Yankee "intellectual" did understand, he would not dare to tell the truth about the South and her oppressed people — not if he wished to maintain his position as a Yankee "intellectual."

At the outbreak of *the War* (1861), an editor for a Northern newspaper declared the North's hatred of the South when he wrote, "We mean to conquer them, Subjugate them...Never would traitors be permitted to return to peaceful and contented homes; instead they must find poverty at their firesides, and see privation in the anxious eyes of mothers and the rags of children." Nor was this opinion held only by a few in the North. President Andrew Johnson, after *the War* was over, declared that Southern traitors "must be punished and impoverished." President Ulysses S. Grant became President after the end of President Andrew Johnson's administration. In President Grant's Inarguable Address, he recognized the deplorable poverty in the conquered South but offered no assistance to the average Southerner.

The South, like Job of the Old Testament, has suffered the loss of wealth, loss of sons and daughters, and loss of physical health. The South, like Job, was once rich by the world's standard, but evil came upon the South, just like it came upon Job. Evil came upon Job, not because he deserved it, but because evil, distress, and disaster are part of human existence. Did the Jews who died in Nazi concentration camps deserve it? Did the over 100 million who died under socialist leaders such as Lenin, Stalin, Mao, or Pol Pot deserve it? No! History teaches us that life is full of tragedy. As Job demonstrated, it is not in avoiding tragedy that we confirm transcendent values, it is not in material pleasures and wealth that we find confirmation in our inner most need for true values of the spirit. For Southerners, these spiritual values are based in our faith in the Divine Lordship of our lives and God's love for each individual. Such values are not confirmed by a life of comfort, ease, and pleasure, a life that never experiences the harshness of tragedy. Our spiritual transcendence is realized by the way in which we endure, persevere, and eventually overcome tragedy — even if that overcoming has to wait for generations. It is this "learned humility" that allows us, as sinful humans, to accept and celebrate our ultimate dependence upon God. I hope Southerners will always remember this lesson, especially, as our material advantages increase. As material wealth increases the temptation to forget or abandon spiritual values also increases. Like Israel of old, if we reject our spiritual inheritance, we commit our people to bondage — bondage to un-Godly world powers.

Which Is Better

More about Aunt Minnie Bell Kennedy Longley

In 1919 the Pearl Valley Baptist Church voted to give Minnie Bell Kennedy a scholarship for schooling to become a Missionary. She spent much of her life working to promote Christian values as a part of the Baptist Home Mission efforts. The family still remembers her as a very pious Christian lady and warrior for the Lord.

Grandmother Kennedy's photo album. Purchased in 1909 for $1.50.

Grandmother Kennedy circa 1926. Two girls may be Aunt Minnie Bell's daughters.

Chapter 9:

THE WAR AND THE ORIGIN OF THE BIBLE BELT

(Photo from MS AG Museum Jackson, MS).

THE SOUTH HAS BEEN known as the Bible-Belt for as long as I can remember. I never questioned why it was called the *Bible-Belt*. Even as a young child, it seemed a perfectly normal term, although I could tell that the term was often used by non-Southerners as if the label *Bible-Belt* was some kind of an insult. Far from being an insult—to me, it seemed to be a complement. It appeared to me to be similar to the way early believers in Jesus Christ were called Christians—some meant it as an insult, while others meant it as a generally accurate description of a group of people connected by a common belief. The same can be said about the use of the label, the *Bible-Belt*, to describe the South—after all, we are the most church going people in the United States. The only non-Southern state that would challenge that is Utah, but otherwise, the *Bible-Belt* signifies *Dixie*, the area of the United States with the most church going folks. As in so many things, when attempting to compare *Dixie* with the rest of the United States, it becomes not so much a comparison but an exercise in contrasting the differences.

In 2014, a nationwide research center published a state by state assessment of religious attitudes. Researchers asked questions such as do you pray daily, do you believe in God with absolute certainty, and do you attend church regularly. The data demonstrated that the South was the most religious section within the United States. For example; 75% of Mississippi citizens pray daily, and not surprisingly, 82% of the state's citizens said that they believe in God with absolute certainty, while 49% of Mississippians attend church regularly. Contrast those numbers with the data from Massachusetts. Only 37% of Massachusetts citizens pray daily, only 40% believe in God with absolute certainty, and only 23% attend church regularly. Vermont, another New England state, reported the lowest church attendance in the United States at 21%, with 33% who pray daily, and 41% who believe in God with absolute certainty.

Another study was done by the same group in 2007 surveying white people in each of the 50 states, asking them if they would describe themselves as a Christian evangelical. The average positive (yes, I am a Christian evangelical) response in the North was 21%, whereas the average positive (yes, I am a Christian evangelical) response in the South was 36%. Every Southern state had a larger percentage of its population who self-described as evangelicals than did the nation as a whole. No doubt the number would have been larger in the South had the researchers included the entire population and not just the white population. Black Southerners have a very long and strong history of church attendance. The finding of the 2007 survey demonstrated that even Southern states that have been flooded with non-Southerners, such as Maryland, Virginia, and Florida, still have a high percentage of its citizens who self-describe as evangelicals.

It is a sad fact of history that when a people are struggling during hard times or when outside tyrants oppress their nation, the people tend to "look to God" for comfort, guidance, and help. But once freedom is won or prosperity returns, these same people (or the next generation) tend to ignore the very God who sustained them during the hard times. I fear that this is happening to the South just as it happened to God's people of Israel, as recorded in the Old Testament. In our day, it is happening to the people of Ireland.

Ireland is a modern-day example of how a people struggling against great odds during hard times and political oppression can lose their religious conviction after the hard times are gone, and material riches flood the land. While the Irish were being oppressed by the

The War and the Origin of the Bible Belt

English Empire, they clung to their faith. The Church was essential in the struggle to maintain the Irish culture. The Church supported the people's earnest and legitimate desire to be free. The Church supported the people's desire to have a government of their own and not be ruled by politicians in London who did not share their Irish religious faith, culture, and traditions. Today, Ireland is free and prosperous. But the Irish have slowly begun to abandon their dedication to the faith that made their freedom and prosperity possible. The young are slowly beginning to take on the belief and immoral values of secular humanism and neo-Marxist postmodernism. This tendency to allow material pleasures to cloud one's vision of freedom and Godliness was captured in a line in a 2002 version of "Scotland the Brave" — the national anthem of Scotland: "Freedom expires amid softness and sighs."

The South has been the target of Northern radical extremists from the very beginning of the United States — especially radical extremists from New England. Donald and I discuss in detail the cultural differences between the North and the South in chapter one of "Yankee Empire: Aggressive Abroad and Despotic at Home." By 1861, when Southern states began seceding from the Union, virtually all Southern Christian Clergy and their congregations had become very suspicious about the type of society the people of the North were establishing in their portion of America. Yankee religious leaders and education centers had abandoned orthodox Christianity and substituted a belief in their ability, through various trendy social fads and "isms," to perfect man and human society. Their aim was to re-make society via government — a central government controlled by Northern (especially New England) political, social, and financial elites. They viewed themselves as a special people who were ordained to compel the rest of America, and eventually, the world to conform to their perverted ideas and "isms," even if it meant compelling submission at the point of bloody bayonets. And of course, being good Yankees, they always made sure to turn a handsome profit during such "conversions" of resistant heathens — heathens being any people who dare to rebel against or resist Yankee rule.

In many respects, Southern religious leaders saw *the War* as a struggle between "powers and principalities." Southern church leaders had always warned their congregations against being over-confident in secular human endeavors to cure actual or perceived evils of the world — the horrors of the French Revolution (1789-90) being a prime example of secular humanism in action. The failure in my day of the Federal government's massive War On Poverty, which began in 1964, is just one of many examples of the cost of human arrogance and conceit that Southern religious leaders foresaw. Trillions of tax dollars have been spent, yet the percentage of the population living in poverty is as bad today as it was back in 1964. Trillions of dollars and volumes of laws, court orders, rules, regulations, and over half a century of tyrannical Federal enforcement bureaucracies have not produced the promised result. What is worse is that the spiritual poverty created in the wake of the War on Poverty has led to the death of hundreds of thousands of the very people the War on Poverty was intended to help — and add to that number the countless thousands of black babies killed via abortion. The founder of the Salvation Army said: "Before you can get the man out of the gutter, you must first get the gutter out of the man." Southern religious leaders have always known that human government is ill-equipped to "get the gutter out of the man." Our Southern ancestors understood this simple, but eternal, truth: Social disaster follows when arrogant man tries to replace God with government.

During the harsh days of *the War*, when food and material supplies were in short supply, Southern soldiers, both *rank and file,* as well as officers, turned to God for support and comfort. In the winter of 1862-64, there were religious services almost every night in Confederate armies. Tens of thousands of Confederate soldiers in the Army of Northern Virginia formed the Army Christian Association. Its purpose was to hold prayer meetings at least three times a week. The same thing was happening in the other Confederate Armies — The Army of the Trans-Mississippi and The Army of Tennessee. These Southern soldiers and their fellow Southerners back home saw *the War* as a dispute between the people of the South who believed in orthodox Christian values as outlined in the Holy Bible and those of the North who proclaimed their own personal moral (ideological) beliefs as being superior to Holy Scripture. The South's unfortunate defeat in 1865 did not change the attitude of Southerners, in fact, it only made them cling with even greater affinity to the Old Rugged Cross.

The religious camp meetings, prayer meetings, and revival meetings held weekly and many times nightly in Confederate camps became the seeds for a religious revival that spread across the South for decades after *the War*. Our entire family would always attend Wednesday night prayer meetings. A tradition that very likely had its origins in the prayer meetings held in Confederate camps during *the War*. Southern scholars, writers, and private citizens have, in differing versions, noted that the Bible-Belt was born of war, nourished by Reconstruction, and matured in subsequent generations who were suffering under Yankee imposed poverty. The Southern soldier was not perfect. As with all humans, he had his faults, but as a whole, there has never been an army actively engaged in war that was more intent upon improving its moral standing before God and man than the Army of the Confederate States of America. When someone asked General Robert E. Lee to expound upon his military exploits, he meekly turned aside from the request and replied, "I can say that I am nothing but a poor sinner trusting in Christ alone for salvation... My chief concern is to try to be an humble, earnest Christian." It is impossible to imagine such words coming from the likes of Yankee Generals, Sherman, Grant, Sheridan, or "Beast" Butler.

Yes, the South is the *Bible-Belt*. She, the South, is home to a people who have suffered the afflictions of Job in the Old Testament but who endured, and to some extent, overcame the unending tragedies of life. The basis of the ability to overcome the tragedies of life, both man-made and natural, was her faith in the Eternal Providence of Almighty God. In her moments of deepest gloom, despair, and oppressions; while her conquerors clapped their hands over her distress and slandered her dead by claiming her sons were traitors who had fought for slavery; while the rest of the United States was seeking worldly pleasures and discarding the moral restraints of Holy Scriptures; and while she was forced on her knees by overwhelming power of a military-industrial empire; she discovered that on her knees was the best place to look up to God with renewed hope for eventual deliverance and ultimate vindication. The South is our mother, and a mother's sons and daughters must always rise to defend their mother.

Today, the South appears to be slouching towards Gomorrah. Just like Israel of Old and Ireland today, the South is beginning the slow but insidious process of discarding the inhibiting restraints of Holy Scripture and our traditional, conservative faith, while it reaches for the glittering illusion of worldly material pleasures. It is a Satanic illusion designed to destroy a Godly people. Beware: Evil never comes to you as an ugly demon, it always presents itself as beautiful, pleasurable, and something that will free you from those "outdated" inhibitions of yesterday. If the South can withstand the siren call of hedonistic materialism, it may well yet be, as Southern author Richard Weaver noted, "The last chance America and the world has to establish a non-materialistic civilization."

"Let's go down to the river to pray." (Photo courtesy of Freedom Valley Old Regular Baptist Church, London, KY).

1930s Sharecropper family singing gospel songs. (Photo courtesy LOC).

Chapter 10:

OUR FAMILY REMEMBERED THE WAR

IT USED TO BE A COMMON saying in the South that while Yankees got their history from Yankee history books written by Yankees, Southerners got their history from their family. Sometime around 1957, when I was 10 years old, the last Confederate veteran died. There was an article about it in the Sunday newspaper. I recall reading it while at my Uncle Lloyd's house (Lloyd Ernest Kennedy 1908-1959). When he saw me reading it, he immediately began telling me about his grandfather, John Wesley Kennedy (1828-1909), who was a Confederate veteran. That would make John Wesley Kennedy, my great grandfather. Dad would often point out John Wesley Kennedy's grave site in the community cemetery—or graveyard, as we would say. There were other community members buried there who were also Confederate veterans. The community graveyard was a place

USS Cairo. (Photo Wikimedia Commons).

where the living showed respect for the dead; where today remembers and honors yesterday; all in the hope that tomorrow, we too will be remembered and honored. I recall seeing an inscription on a grave marker in one of the hundreds of cemeteries I have visited across the South that said: "Where you are now, I once was—where I am now, you one day will be." Something all of us should keep in mind.

It was a few years after the last Confederate veteran died, that the state of Mississippi raised the *USS Cairo* from the bottom of the Yazoo River. The Yazoo River is just north of Vicksburg, Mississippi. The *USS Cairo* was sunk by a Confederate underwater mine placed in the river by Confederate forces. The sunken Yankee warship was raised, put on a barge, and floated down river to Vicksburg. Some brave Southerner caused a lot of distress in Yankeeland when he placed a Confederate flag on the bow of the barge carrying the *USS Cairo*! No one down South thought it was wrong—after all, we sunk it, we raised it, and we were bringing it down river on our barge. It was given to the U. S. Park Service at Vicksburg, where it remains today as a tribute to the brave men on both sides who perished in that most unnecessary of wars—a war initiated by Lincoln and his co-conspirators to keep Southern revenues flowing into Yankee hands.

Uncle Lloyd told us that our great grandfather was stationed in a rifle-pit (a modern-day army would call it a fox hole) when the *USS Cairo* was sunk. Uncle Lloyd told us that the mine (during *the War* mines were called torpedoes) that sunk the Yankee gunboat was made by skilled black craftsmen in Yazoo City, Mississippi. As a young boy, I never thought to question these family stories. They were part of our family's oral history. Years later, while researching, Donald and I found our great grandfather Kennedy's parole papers that were issued after the surrender of Vicksburg. Sure enough, he had been in the trenches or rifle pits on the banks of the Mississippi River, serving with the 38th Mississippi Infantry, CSA, when the *USS Cairo* was sent to the bottom of the Yazoo River. The sinking of the *USS Cairo* was the first time that a United States Naval war vessel was sunk by an underwater mine. While doing research I also found an old United Confederate Veteran magazine article that described the sinking of the *USS Cairo*. The article's author stated that black craftsmen constructed many of these torpedoes. Family history verified! This is an example of how important oral history is to a family. A Confederate veteran told a story to his grandson (Uncle Lloyd Kennedy) who then passed the story on to his nephews (Donald and I)—the Confederate veteran's great grandsons. And now, I pass it on to you.

Uncle Lloyd also told about how, in 1866 (a year after the end of *the War*), when a steamboat company was building a fancy new steamboat on the Yankee side of the Ohio River. The local folks in New Albany,

Indiana, would take bets on what the builders would name the new riverboat. It almost caused a riot when these fine Yankees saw the name being painted on the steamboat was none other than Robert E. Lee. The owners had to protect the boat by quickly floating the steamboat across the Ohio River and dock it on the Kentucky side near Louisville, Kentucky. Uncle Lloyd thought this was funny. But he said that the Yankee's way of thinking has not changed much because when "Gone With the Wind" opened in Chicago in 1940, they almost had an anti-South riot there as well — all because of a movie that dared to say charming things about the South!

Uncle Lloyd was not the only family member who told us stories about *the War*. I recall Great Aunt Vivian telling us about her uncle (or maybe it was her cousin-my memory fades) who served in the Confederate army. We spent a fair amount of time visiting with Aunt Vivian. She lived about a quarter of a mile down the road. She was our Grandmother Berry's (1890-1972) sister who had married my Grandfather Kennedy's brother, Great Uncle Charlie Kennedy (1871-1948). Aunt Vivian said that her Uncle died after the first day of a two-day battle. He was sitting on a log, eating his meager rations, when he fell over dead. The family thought he most likely died of a heart attack. She said that he was too old to be in the army, but he joined up anyway. He was a simple farmer too old for the rigors of military life. He was not part of the plantation system, just a simple farmer. Yet, modern day, politically correct "scholars" insist on slandering his good name by claiming that he was fighting for slavery. No, he and his comrades were fighting for the same thing their Colonial forefathers fought for back in 1776 —

Uncle Lloyd in his corn field — cotton in background. Note bib overalls, long sleeve shirt and broad brim hat, circa 1955.

My Berry Grandparents. Walter and Naomi Berry, circa 1950.

the right to establish a government of their own based upon their free and unfettered consent. This basic American right is described in the 1776 Declaration of Independence as an inalienable right; "the consent of the governed." By the way, don't forget that in 1776 when the American colonies were fighting for independence, slavery was legal in every colony, and the New England colonies were actively engaged in the nefarious international slave trade. If slavery was not a reason to deny that the colonies had a just cause in 1776, then the same is true of the South in 1861.

Our Grandfather Berry told us about his grandfather, who also served in the Confederate Army. He was assigned to the 36th Mississippi Infantry that fought at the Siege of Port Hudson on the Mississippi River just north of Baton Rouge, Louisiana. I always thought it was interesting that our Great Grandfather Kennedy was fighting at the Siege of Vicksburg on the Mississippi River while at the same time our Great, Great, Grandfather Berry was fighting at the Siege of Port Hudson on the Mississippi River in Louisiana. Even though they did not know each other, they were comrades defending their country — the Confederate States of America. They were defending their right to live in a country of their own, a country based upon the free and unfettered consent of the governed. It is an inalienable right that may be suppressed but never destroyed.

I recall a time when Grandmother Berry (1890-1972), Great Aunt Vivian Kennedy and Mom (1917-2006) were visiting. Donald and I wanted to watch TV because that was the night that "The Gray Ghost: Mosby's Rangers" came on. *Back in the day*, it was not considered evil to tell the truth about the South and *the War*. The TV program Mosby's Rangers would open with a scene showing the Confederate cavalry riding their horses with a Confederate Battle Flag proudly flying. When the TV program took a commercial break, I asked Grandma — with the innocence of a young child — "Grandma, where do Yankees come from?" All conversation ceased as everyone sat in silence to hear Grandma's answer. "Lord have mercy, son," she declared. "I can't tell you that. All I can say is that they *ain't* us!" Mom and Aunt Vivian laughed at her response to my childish question. The thing that has stuck in my mind all the years since then was not Grandma's answer but the laughter that came from Mom and Aunt Vivian. It was not the kind of laughter that you hear when someone tells a funny story. It was more in the nature of a nervous laughter. It was the kind of laughter you would get when someone tries to lighten a tense situation by making a humorous but polite comment. I think they knew more than they could say, more than they knew how to say. They knew that something terrible had been inflected upon their *people* — their *kith and kin* — across the South, but they had no way to express their sense of grief and remorse. Sometimes, it is just better to laugh than to cry.

Chapter 11:

UNCLE FRANK SMITH: SNAKE HANDLER AND COUNTRY PHILOSOPHER

DAD'S YOUNGEST SISTER, Hattie, married a poor young man, Frank Smith, from a neighboring community. Aunt Hattie (1902-1986) and Uncle Frank Smith (1904-1968) lived on the land that was Aunt Hattie's inheritance of Granddaddy Kennedy's land. They built a small cabin and raised one son. Their son, we called him Little Frankie, would eventually join that great Southern mass migration out of the impoverished South to the steel mills of the North in search for jobs unavailable in the economically depressed South. Uncle Frank was one of those characters in my life that made life interesting and from whom I learned a lot about how to enjoy life in the rural South.

Uncle Frank was known for his ability to kill snakes by grabbing their tail, whirling the snake over his head like a cowboy's lasso, and then, as if he were cracking a bullwhip, he would crack the snake's head off. By whirling the snake over his head like a lasso, he created a centrifugal force that made it impossible for the snake to reach back and bite his hand. After whirling the snake over his head for a while, he would then snap it like cracking a bull whip and off would fly the snake's head. This process was demonstrated at church one Sunday morning—much to the delight of all the boys. Just before church was to begin, several of the girls started screaming—the kind of scream you know immediately that it means danger or trouble. Uncle Frank and several of us boys were first on the scene. There was a large rattle snake slithering up the steps to the church's side door. The snake already had its head across the door's threshold. Uncle Frank sprang into action, warning us to "git back!" In one swoop, he grabbed the snake's tail and began whirling it over his head. With a quick whip action, the rattle snake's head flew off. Uncle Frank then turned to us and declared, "Ole Satan thought he was a going to sneak into the Lord's House and cause some mischief—you boys got to always watch out for Ole Satan; he'll sneak up on you when you least expect it." Amen, Uncle Frank, Amen!

Donald and I would watch Uncle Frank plow his corn and cotton crops in his field next to our house. He never seemed to be in a hurry. Slow and steady was his motto. He would be out in his field plowing before we were out of bed in the morning. At noon, he would take his mule back to his barn, draw water from his well to water the mule, give the mule a few nubbins (small ears of corn), wash the plow dirt off his face and hands, and promptly, at high noon, he would eat *dinner*. He used to tell us, "Boys, when I'm standing and look down to see by my shadow that I'm a standing on my head—it's time to eat!" There was no such thing as *"lunch"* on a farm—we ate *dinner* at noon and *supper* in the evening. After eating his *dinner*, he would take a nap until around 2 PM because that was the hottest part of the day. While plowing, he always wore a slouch-hat with a broad brim to shield his face from the sun and a long-sleeved work shirt to shield his arms from the sun. Donald and I asked Dad why Uncle Frank always wore long sleeve shirts even during hot summer days. Dad explained that old folks always protected their white skin from the sun to prevent skin cancer when they got old. He told us that we should at least wear a hat to protect our head and face. Well, that was too old fashioned for us! Today, we both make regular trips to the dermatologist to make sure our skin that was over-exposed to the sun in our youth does not result in skin cancer in our old age. I swear, every time the doctor freezes a "dangerous looking spot" off my head, I can hear Dad up in Heaven, saying, "See I told you so."

Aunt Hattie Kennedy Smith and Uncle Frank Smith, circa 1960.

Uncle Frank Smith

Uncle Frank had a unique system for putting out ammonia nitrate, which is a form of fertilizer chemically composed of the nitrate salt of the ammonium cation. *Back in the day*, it was very common just to call it soda. The process of dispensing the ammonium nitrate was called "dropping soda." Just prior to *laying-by* the corn crop, the farmer would drop soda, and then using a turning-plow, "bar off" the row. This would throw a small amount of dirt from the trench between the rows on to the row with the corn plant. This would be done for the entire field. It would leave a "bar" or a long stretch of dirt three to four inches wide in the trench between each row. Then, using a plow called a middle-buster, the farmer "runs the middle," which takes the dirt from the bar in the middle trench between the rows and throughs it right and left up on and around the corn stalks, covering the soda. Some farmers would use a six-inch shovel stock with a hill sweep attached to run the middles when *laying by* their crop. A good rain within a week or two after the crop was *laid-by* would assure an excellent fall harvest.

Dad taught us to "drop soda" by walking between the rows (walking in the trench between the rows) carrying the soda in a galvanized three-gallon bucket. We would reach down into the bucket, grab a small amount of soda, between a quarter and a half cup, and then drop it next to but not on the corn stalk. If you drop it on the corn stalk, it will burn the tender plant. Uncle Frank was far more precise. He would take a table spoon, scoop the soda out of his bucket, lightly shake the spoon to level the fertilizer in the spoon, and gently spread it around the plant no closer than about three fingers width. It took him a lot longer to drop soda than it did us. Even though he used less soda than we did, his crop always looked just as good. He would admonish Dad that we were wasting expensive soda. The difference was that Dad did not have the week days to work our fields. We had to get the *laying-by* done on a Saturday because Dad worked during the weekdays. And of course, there was never even a thought of working on the Lord's Day—Sunday. Sunday was a holy day reserved for going to church and Sunday school in the morning and to Training Union and church that night. After *dinner* we would spend the day visiting our Grandfather and Grandmother Berry and playing with our cousins on Mom's side of the family.

For a long while, the only heat in the house was from our fire places. We had two, one in the master bedroom and one in the living room. It would usually take two wagon loads of firewood to heat the house through the winter. To get the most heat from your firewood, it needs to dry during the summer. If you run out of dry firewood and have to cut more to get you through the rest of the winter, it will be "green wood," meaning that it is full of sap. When green firewood is burned in the fireplace, you can actually see the sap oozing out of the cut ends of the wood. We always said that it took two dry sticks of firewood to burn one green stick. It is always best to cut firewood late in the winter or early in spring before plowing time arrives and allow it to dry over the summer.

The wood cut from the tree trunk will need to be split into "sticks of firewood" small enough to use in the fireplace. This requires the use of metal wedges that are driven into the block of wood by a sledge hammer. It takes considerable skill to first know where on the cut end of the block to place the wedge and then to be able to swing the sledge hammer with force, striking the wedge evenly on the "head" of the wedge. The test to determine if your firewood is dry is to take two sticks and knock them together. If they are dry, they will produce a high pitched almost metallic sound. If they are still wet, they will make a low pitched "thud" sound.

Dad would get Uncle Frank to help him cut down a hardwood tree, usually an oak, that Dad would select. The bottom land next to Peggy Creek grew many fine hardwoods. Dad was always careful to select trees that would not be good for logging. Logs would be another source of cash for the family. I recall that we sold logs from the bottom land twice while living at home. By the time Donald and I were nine or ten years old, we were expected to help load, unload, and stack the firewood. Uncle Frank's mule and our mule, Ole Jeff, were hitched together as a team to pull the wagon. We always enjoyed riding the wagon down to the bottom land. Uncle Frank always took the long way to the place where the cut wood was on the ground waiting for us to load it on the wagon. He took the long route in order to have the wagon wheels role through as many ditches filled with water as possible. This was because the wagon wheels were made of wood with an iron rim fitted around the wooden circumference. The wood would dry and shrink when not in use. This would cause the wheel spokes to loosen and possibly fall out, or the metal rim around the wheel could fall off. Uncle Frank knew this and would always make sure he "watered the wagon wheels" any time he hitched up a wagon.

On one occasion, while we were loading the wagon, I became concern about whether the mules would be able to pull the load. I voiced my concern to Dad and Uncle Frank that perhaps we were putting too much work on the mules. Uncle Frank's reply was to laughed out loud and declare, "Just *load the wagon boys, don't worry about the mules, just load the wagon!*" Of course, from many years of experience, they knew how much the mules could pull. That bit of country advice has stuck with Donald and I all our lives. Often when working with volunteer organizations, such as the Sons of Confederate Veterans, even though we are working diligently on a volunteer project, we would have members come to us and tell us that we should do *"thus-and-such"* or add an extra step to the project we are working on. Of course, they were not volunteering to help us with the project, they just wanted us to do more. We would look at each other and in unison, declare, *"Just load the wagon boys, don't worry about the mules!"*

I don't think Uncle Frank ever finished high school. But that did not stop him from reading old newspapers when the neighbors were finished with them. He kept up with world affairs—I think more to assure himself that the world was headed in the wrong direction than to gain knowledge of current affairs. He could see and would often declare to anyone who would listen, that a rich and materialistic world is more likely to be spiritually impoverished. "What good is it for a man to gain the whole world but lose his soul," he would often say, quoting Jesus from Matthew 16:26. He was a self-taught scholar in things of the Bible. I recall seeing him many a day after eating *dinner*, sitting in the swing on the front porch of his small cabin, reading his Bible. He would be quick to challenge the preacher or Sunday School teacher on scriptural interpretation or church doctrine. He lived a simple life but was always available to "lend a helping hand." I know of widow women who would go to Uncle Frank when they needed someone to loan them money. He would lend them the cash and tell them to "pay it back when you can." They always did, and he never thought of charging interest. He was not a banker. He did not trust banks. Every dollar he had, all his worldly possessions, was tied up in his simple cabin, farming implements, old pick-up truck, and cash stored in a mason jar on the shelf in the kitchen. He never locked the door to his house. *Back in the day*, none of us locked the doors of our house or took the key out of the car's ignition when we parked our car in town. The politically correct, neo-Marxist, progressive, enemies of the conservative, *Bible-Belt*, South claim that those were evil days—you be the judge.

Uncle Frank taught us several country sayings that have proven to be useful to us. One was a way to identify poison ivy and not confuse it with Virginia Creeper. As Uncle Frank taught us, "Leaves of three, leave be (leave them alone); leaves of five, let thrive." Poison ivy has three leaves whereas Virginia Creeper, which is often confused with poison ivy, has five leaves and a saw tooth edge on its five leaves. Another country saying is one that was sadly brought to mind lately (2019) when the local St. Tammany Parish news related a story of a man who died from a snake bite. It seems that the man wanted to show his friends a relatively rare form of the harmless Kingsnake—the Scarlet Kingsnake. This rare Kingsnake has red, black, and yellow stripes, and is very beautiful (as far as snakes go—I don't like snakes). Unfortunately, there is also a very venomous snake that is also a rarity in the lower South—the Coral snake. It too has red, black and yellow stripes. Its toxin is a neurotoxin—it interferes with the transmission of nerve signals from the brain to the cardiac and respiratory muscles. It can take as long as twelve hours after a bite before the victim begins to have symptoms. The poor fellow did not know the difference and received several bites from what he thought was a kingsnake but was actually a Coral snake. He died the next day. Uncle Frank told us to remember, "Red on yellow will kill a fellow, red on black good luck jack." The Scarlet Kingsnake has red bands that touch black bands ("red on black, good luck Jack"), while the Coral snake has red bands that touch yellow bands ("red on yellow will kill a fellow").

One beautiful Sunday in 1968, Brother Douglass announced at the closing of church services that there would be a meeting of the men folk at the community cemetery (we always called it the graveyard) at 2:30 that afternoon. They would make plans for a Saturday work day to clean the cemetery and fix the fence. The community cemetery is located about three miles to the east of our home. It sits not far from the bank of Peggy Creek and about a mile from the Pearl River. The road that goes in front of our house and the church leads to the cemetery. The road crosses Mississippi Highway 27. As I was leaving church that Sunday, Uncle Frank hollered at me, "Boy, you want to ride with me down to the meeting this afternoon?" I had planned to leave early and drive back to Vicksburg, Mississippi, where I worked as the Head of the Respiratory Therapy Department at Mercy Hospital. I told Uncle Frank I was not sure if I would still be around for the meeting. His reply was, "Well, boy, if you are and want to ride with me, just meet me down at the fork of the road." The fork of the road was about 50 yards down from our house. When time for the meeting came, I had become involved in reading a book. I was sitting on the side porch where I could see the fork of the road. I saw Uncle Frank slow down, looked around, and not seeing me, he drove off in his 1948 Chevrolet pick-up truck.

Dad told me that when they finished down at the cemetery, Uncle Frank told the gathering that we had better take care of the cemetery and keep our souls in order because we never know who will be the next person we put in the ground. A little over an hour after seeing Uncle Frank drive off toward the cemetery, as I was getting ready to leave for Vicksburg, I heard the squealing of tires and a loud crash coming from the direction of Highway 27. Uncle Frank had pulled out in front of a car going north on Highway 27. Unable to stop, the car plowed into the driver's side of Uncle Franks' pick-up truck, killing him instantly. With great sadness, we cleaned the cemetery and had it ready to receive the earthly remains of its next citizen. We made sure the cemetery was clean, and I am sure Uncle Frank had his soul

Uncle Frank Smith

Uncle Frank Smith inspired the creation of Uncle Seth telling his Great-Grandchildren stories about the War. (C. Whittington, artist).

in order—the final bit of wisdom Uncle Frank taught me, and I pass it alone to you. I feel very blessed to have lived in the days when giants walked the earth, disguised as poor Southern farmers.

Years later, I was thinking about writing a historical fiction based on first-hand accounts of Southern civilians and soldiers during *the War*. I was perplexed or possibly had a form of writer's block. I wanted to tell these true stories, but I was unsure how to tell these unconnected short stories. I had researched and collected a lot of personal accounts, but they were not connected as in a novel. I hit on the idea of having a fictitious old Confederate veteran tell these stories to his fictitious grandchildren and great grandchildren. All the stories are true, but the individual telling the stories and his family are fictional. But when you create a fictitious character, you need to give him a unique personality, or else, he is only a name on the page. As a writer you want your fictitious character to come alive in the reader's mind. I knew immediately that Uncle Frank would be my model for my fictitious story-teller. The fictitious story-teller I created is Uncle Seth and the book is "Uncle Seth Fought the Yankees." Uncle Seth's personality is the mirror image of Uncle Frank. I am personally acquainted with a fictitious character, a character conjured up in my own imagination. He is not a real person, but to me, he is real. I know Uncle Seth personally because I knew Uncle Frank.

Mule pulled turning-plow.
Note board and batten construction used on outbuilding wall. (Photo LOC).

Chapter 12:

LOGGING WITH OX TEAMS

OUR GRANDFATHER BERRY (Walter Berry 1890-1972) told us about his favorite team (yoke) of oxen he used to haul logs out of swamps and bottom lands—the term he used was "skidding logs." Today, logging is still hard and dangerous work, but most of the physical work today is done by machines. *Back in the day*, it was done mostly by human and animal labor. Trees would be cut down using a cross-cut saw. The saw had a handle on each end, a pair of men would work together, each holding one of the handles and take turns pulling the saw toward himself. It required a bit of practice to gain the skill necessary to get into and keep a good rhythm of pulling the saw back and forth. After the tree was cut down or "fell," loggers would use double bladed axes to trim the larger limbs off the tree trunk, mark the log for length of cut—usually between ten to twenty feet—and then, they would use the cross-cut saw to cut the tree trunk into logs. Each log could weigh a few hundred pounds to several tons. Remember, this was back in the day before there were tractors. Every log had to be moved from the cutting site to the loading site and then loaded onto a log wagon by physical effort—human and animal. Some loggers used logging mules, which were much larger and stronger than the standard mule used for

Five yoke of oxen pulling log wagon. Note no bridle or reins used to guide oxen. The drover gives commands by voice and bull whip. Photo from Kennedy family album.

Jacob Summerlin, Florida, circa 1870s. He was known as the "King of the Crackers". (Photo courtesy of the State Archives of Florida).

plowing. But Granddaddy Berry preferred to use a yoke of oxen because they were easier to control and would pull the heavy logs through deep mud. Mules would bulk and jump out of the trace-chains when they got into deep mud. Oxen, on the other hand, would actually get on their knees while pulling the log through deep mud.

My Great Uncle James S. Little (1906-2000), Grandmother Berry's youngest brother, told me he remembered seeing settlers coming into Simpson County (this would have been before Simpson County was officially organized as a county). He said the settlers traveled in covered wagons pulled by teams (yokes) of oxen. Oxen move slower than mules or horses, but they are steady and can pull heavy loads much longer. The teamster is the person who drives the team of animals. The correct term for the oxen teamster is drover. When my Great Grandfather John Wesley Kennedy (1828-1909) joined the 38th Mississippi Infantry at the outbreak of *the War*, he was mustered in as a teamster. A lot of Yankee "scholars" claim that if blacks served in the Confederate Army, they only served as teamsters, cooks, and such. But in all armies, it takes a lot more soldiers filling support roles than those who are on the front line of battle. But black Southerners served not only in support roles, but as combat soldiers as well.

Driving yokes of oxen requires different equipment (harness) and skills than needed for driving teams of horses or mules. For horses and mules, the teamster must use reins attached to bridles to guide horses or mules. The bridle has a metal "bit" that is placed in the horse/mule's mouth that allows (compels) the animal to respond to a pull

Logging with Ox Teams

on the reins—pull left to go left, pull right to go right. The stronger the pull the sharper the animal is trained to turn. When turning the team right, the teamster will give the command *gee*, and when turning left, the command *haw* is given. A well-trained team will often turn right or left at the mere sound of gee or haw. I should note that the bridle bit used and the technique for "reining" the animal is different for draft horses than for riding horses. The technique for "driving" oxen, on the other hand, is completely different. Yokes of oxen do not have bridles and bits; the teamster (drover) does not use any reins at all! The drover uses a bull whip to signal to the oxen which direction to turn. The bullwhip is not used to whip the animals, but the cracking sound made by the bullwhip is all the signal the oxen need. The drover will crack his whip on the right side, and the animals will turn in the opposite direction (left), or crack the whip on the left side to get the animals to turn right.

Back in the day, no one thought about what caused the bullwhip's cracking sound. But after the turn of the jet-age *redneck* theories developed as to what caused the cracking sound. The cracking sound made by a bullwhip was thought to be caused by the tip of the whip breaking the sound bearer and causing a mini sonic boom. More recent scientific studies have discovered that it is not the tip of the whip but the loop that indeed breaks the sound bearer and causes the crack or mini sonic boom. Think about that—your teamster (drover) great, great, grandfathers were breaking the sound bearer long before man could fly!

The *Scotch-Irish* settlers who moved into the Southern backcountry used oxen as their main draft animals. Horses were saddled and ridden by the men while women and children rode in the ox-wagon, or they walked. Walking was a relief from bumping over rough ground in wagons with iron rimed wheels and no springs. Spanish officials in Florida (before Florida became part of the United States) referred to these *Scotch-Irish* settlers who were

Grandfather Walter Berry and his yoke of Oxen, circa 1920. Photo from Kennedy family album.

moving from southern Georgia into northern Florida as *"Crackers"* because of the cracking sound of their bull whips. From 1901 to 1965, there was a minor league baseball team in Georgia named the Atlanta Crackers. The term *"Crackers"* has been inappropriately turned into a derogatory and belittling word by politically correct folks. They have often made the claim that white Southerners are called *"Crackers"* because our ancestors cracked whips on slaves. This is just one of innumerable examples of slander and lies heaped upon the South, and we, the people of a conquered nation, have no means to appropriately respond. We have no way to correct the lies heaped upon our people by the politically correct crowd who are pushing their left of center political agenda.

Isn't it strange that in today's politically correct America, we are warned against using any words to describe a group of people if that word or term might be considered offensive? Often these hyper-sensitive millennials are called "snowflakes." They even demand that we surrender our right of free speech. Yet, the politically correct crowd find it perfectly OK to heap derision upon Southerners by using terms such as "crackers," "rednecks," and "hillbillies" to describe folks who do not agree with their leftwing ideology. In today's America, everyone has rights except traditional, conservative, God fearing, Southerners. Is this truly a nation "with liberty and justice for all?"

Chapter 13:

HOG-KILLING TIME
MEAT FOR SUPPER RAISED ON THE FARM

IN THE EARLY 1950s, Southern comedians told a joke that very few today would understand—the humor would be lost on most modern Southerners. The joke is set in the 1950s. It was the era before air-conditioning which did not become common in homes, stores, and especially cars until the late-1960s. The joke was that a rich Yankee was driving down South during the late summer in his new air-conditioned car. He saw a poor farmer walking in the heat and decided to give the farmer a ride. The farmer was shocked when he sat down in the cool car. The Yankee asked the farmer where he was going. The farmer replied, "I was headed to the store to get a new pair of brogans (ankle high leather work boots worn by farmers), but now that this cold front has come through, I think I will head back home and kill some hogs." This was hilarious to Southerners of that time, but today, it fails as comedy because very few people know about "hog-killing time" or life in the hot South before air-conditioning.

Today, when a family decides to serve ham for *supper*, where do they get the meat? (Remember, in the South, *dinner* is the noon meal, while *supper* is the last meal of the day. As we often remind folks "The Lord Jesus did not have the last *dinner*—he had the Last Supper.") When modern folks want meat for *supper*, they go to the store to carefully select and purchase a neatly wrapped cut of meat. But in our time in the rural South, it was common to raise your own hogs and beef cattle and slaughter the animals yourself. "Hog-killing time" was always done when the weather was very cold because there was no other way to freeze or even refrigerate a whole animal. You slaughtered your animals when it was cold because the meat would *keep* while you were processing (cutting up the different parts), and no flies would be around to ruin the meat.

I remember the old smoke house that was still in use when Donald and I were three or four years old. The meat was packed in salt and placed (hung) in the smoke house where a constant smoldering fire

The Kennedy wash pot used during hog killing time.

was kept. The smoke from dried hickory, pecan, or oak logs gave the meat a good smoked flavor and helped to cure the meat. Insects and meat-eating animals would not venture into the smoke. It usually took two days for hams to "cure" and up to six days for a brown crust to cover the cured meat. The smoke house walls sat on the ground. The floor was pure red clay. The "ground seal" or hewed logs that supported the walls sat directly on the ground. The "ground seals" were pure heart pine so full of *rosin* that they would not rot or be attacked by termites. Over time, the dirt (clay) floor collected a lot of the salt that fell from the curing meat. Our Great Aunt Vivian Kennedy said that her parents told her that during *the War* and afterwards, the only source for salt that starving Southerners had was obtained from the dirt from smokehouse floors. They, like most Southerners after *the War*, were too poor to purchase large, 50 to 100-pounds bags of salt. She said her father and mother told her about how they would dig-up the dirt floor, put the salty dirt in wash pots, pour off the salty water, and boil it down to get the salt. Such was the poverty of the defeated and occupied South. Salt, in a hot humid climate, is an essential for human survival.

Hog-killing time usually involved several neighbors. Slaughtering and preparing a whole animal in one day took a lot of work. Having helpful neighbors was a necessity. Uncle Frank Smith brought his .22-caliber rifle to shoot the hog. Dad only had his father's double barrel shotgun, and a shotgun with its many pellets would ruin the meat. Uncle Frank's rifle's one bullet did the job nicely. Uncle Frank always used a .22-caliber short bullet, never a larger size, or hollow-point bullet.

A large, black wash-pot was filled with water, dried oak firewood stacked around it, and the water brought to a "rolling boil." Mom used heart pine—called *fat lighter*—to start the fire, but she always waited until the fire consumed all the pine before starting the cooking process. The smoke from the pine tainted the lard that was cooked in the wash pot. Folks back in the day knew that different types of wood had different usage—a knowledge few possess today.

The men folk took buckets filled with boiling hot water from the wash pot and poured it on the dead hog, and then, using very sharp butcher knives, they scraped the hair off the animal's body. Beef cattle were skinned and the hide turned into leather, but hogs were scrapped clean of all hair. The hairless hog carcass was then hung up by its hind legs from a *single-tree* and allowed to bleed clean. Seeing all of this at an early age gave us an appreciation for the work necessary to put food on the table. Today, in our "modern" society, we are removed from all of this—as if some machine automatically produces the meat necessary to make our hamburgers, etc.

Another reason to have the neighbors over to help during hog-killing time was that we had no way of freezing the meat. Mom and Dad followed the custom of giving away portions of the meat to those who helped and to elderly or shut-in neighbors (we were in the 7th grade before Mom and Dad could afford to purchase a small freezer). Because people slaughtered their animals at different times during the fall and winter, someone was always giving away small portions of meat to their neighbors. Giving away small portions of a freshly slaughtered animal was necessary to prevent the meat from spoiling, but it also was a way to acknowledge and confirm our neighborly alliances—our mutual dependence on our *kith and kin*. The term "*kith and kin*" is an old *Scotch-Irish* term meaning friends and neighbors as well as those who are your blood kin (relatives).

After all the boiling water was used, the old cast iron wash pot was readied for another part of the day's work. It was used to cook-down the hog fat and process it into lard. The men cut off the hog fat and the women cooked it in the wash pot. The adults managed the process very skillfully. As the fat cooked, it slowly began to float in the boiling liquid (melted) fat. Skill was necessary to know when to take the floating "cracklings" out of the boiling liquid. Once boiled down, the liquid hog fat was poured into a new, five-gallon, tin bucket and allowed to cool. When cool, the fat turned into pure white lard and was used during the year for cooking. The cracklings were kept to eat as a snack (similar to "pig skins" that are commercially available next to the potato chips in many Southern stores today). They were also used to make "crackling bread." The cracklings were crushed and mixed into cornbread batter.

A very telling incident occurred one day during the early 1950s during the annual hog-killing when Donald and I were three or four years old. Mom and Aunt Jeanie, (the black neighbor, who along with her husband—whose name I do not recall—helped during hog killing time). In those days, whites called elderly black women aunt and elderly black men uncle. It was a term of respect that is lost to us today. Although, a reminder of those days remains in Southern grocery stores, such as labels on Aunt Jemima's pancake mix and Uncle Ben's rice. I recall going into the store in Oma, Mississippi, with Dad when Donald and I were only four or five years old. As we entered the store an elderly black man sat outside the store on the *loafers' bench*. Dad spoke to the man, "Good morning, uncle." The man replied with a smile on his face, "Morning, sir (pronounced sur)." I asked Dad, "Is he our uncle?" Dad laughed and said, "No, not a real uncle, but out of respect, we always call elderly black men uncle."

Cooking down the hog fat required a hot fire, and Mom did not want the three-year-old twins around the danger. I recall Aunt Jeanie (now that I think about it, I'm not sure that was her name) telling us boys to stay away from the fire because this fire "would really hurt you boys—yawl stay away from the fire and this hot wash pot." Dad was busy helping the men but was also supposed to keep an eye on the twins. After a short while, Mom noticed that the twins were nowhere to be found and asked Dad where the boys were. Dad thought we were over by the cows, but the cows were gone—it was their habit to head down to the creek to get water early in the morning. Everything stopped! Visions of two little boys drowning in the creek flooded everyone's minds. Uncle Frank tore off (another way of saying he took off or left in a hurry) toward the deepest part of the creek, Dad followed the cow trail, and Mom searched around the house. Aunt Jeanie could not leave the boiling fat, but as she walked around the boiling wash pot, stirring the hog fat and cracklings, she continued to pray out loud, "Oh, Lord Jesus, please protect those little white boys! Lord, don't let them drown in that ole creek. Lord, you knows I can't leave these cracklings, or I'd be out there a looking for them myself." Aunt Jeanie never stopped walking around that pot, stirring the cracklings and praying. Dad found us a short distance from the creek. We followed the cows and almost made it to the creek. As soon as Dad

Hog-Killing Time

found us, he hollered back to the house, and above all the commotion, you could hear Aunt Jeanie shouting, "Praise the Good Lord for all His mercies—those little boys are found—thank you, Jesus!" No doubt, we would have followed the cows into the creek and most likely drowned in the process. I will always believe that prayers were answered that day, and none were more sincerely or fervently prayed than that of an elderly black lady who was part of our *kith and kin*. The Bible instructs us that, "The prayers of the righteous availeth much" (James 5: 16). I look forward to seeing Aunt Jeanie in Heaven, putting my arms around her, and thanking her for her fervent prayers.

Several years later, when Donald and I were around twelve years old, we were given brand new bicycles for Christmas. They were special treats. Before getting our new bikes, we had old hand-me-down "girls'" bikes. Mom decided to send us on a bicycle mission to take Aunt Jeanie her butcher knife that she left while helping at that year's annual hog killing. Aunt Jeanie lived ten to twelve miles from our home, but Mom told us to jump on our bicycles and take Aunt Jeanie's butcher knife back to her. The road in front of our house was paved by then. So, part of the way, the road was paved, but the other half was an old-fashioned gravel road. In those days, it was not uncommon for boys on bicycles to go riding around the community for miles without any concern about their safety. We knew everyone in the community, and they knew us. During that time, there was no concern about "strangers" harming children. If a "stranger" came into the community, people took notice. If he lingered around, the men folk politely asked him what his business was, and if he had no real business in the community, they graciously volunteered to help him find his way out of the community. Also, word about a stranger lurking around was spread to neighboring communities. So, parents were not concerned about their children's safety, and therefore, we spent most of our days during the summer outside and out of sight.

The trip to Aunt Jeanie's home took us about two hours there and two hours back. As we were leaving Aunt Jeanie's home, we met a black boy about our age riding his bicycle. We stopped to talk. He was impressed with our new bikes. Donald offered to let him ride his new bicycle. So, they exchanged bikes and we all rode around for *a spell* (a spell means a short while). I don't recall his name, and we never saw him again. I've often wondered how life turned out for that young boy. It was also the last time I recall seeing Aunt Jeanie. By the time we were twelve or thirteen, Mom and Dad purchased a freezer, and we bought and froze our year's supply of meat—hog-killing time was over for our family. Without realizing it, an important episode of our lives came to a close, but the fond memories will last forever.

Kennedy meat grinder used during hog killing time.

Kennedy sausage stuffer used during hog killing time.

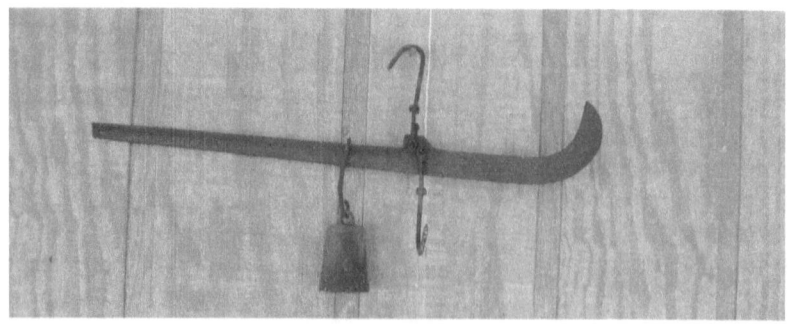

Kennedy cotton scales used to weigh cotton and other farm products.

Chapter 14:

PLOWING THE RED CLAY HILLS OF MISSISSIPPI

WE GREW UP ON A typical "forty *acre* and a mule" farm in the rural South (actually it was forty-five acres). The children were expected to "lend a hand" with chores as soon as we became old enough to handle simple chores. Shelling corn and feeding the chickens were two of the first tasks a young boy might learn. Girls would have tasks assigned to them by their mothers. We did not have a sister, although our first cousins on Dad's side lived just up the road from us and were as close to us as sisters — Dad had all boys and Uncle Lloyd had all girls. By the time we were ten years old, we had mastered the art of hoeing the garden without cutting more vegetable plants than weeds! Eventually, depending on the boy's physical size, he was trained in the skill of plowing the fields. We grew corn and occasionally cotton. Both crops required a lot of plowing to prepare the land for planting, to plant the crop, to plow out weeds, and eventually to *lay-by* the crop.

L. R. James, Carroll County, MS, typical 1950s Southern farmer. Note bib overalls, slouch hat, long sleeve shirt, & brogans.

As young boys, we took notice of how our Uncle

Ronald and Donald Kennedy circa 1992 "Civil War" re-enactors, 12th LA Inf. C.S.A. Photo taken in Magnolia Cemetery Baton Rouge, LA.

Frank plowed his fields. During the hottest days of summer, he always wore a long-sleeved shirt, a large- brimmed hat (called a slouch hat by Southern soldiers during the War), bibbed overalls, and *brogans* (ankle high leather work boots). He would often tie a cord around the bottom of his overall legs below his ankle to keep the dirt out of his *brogans*. During the War, soldiers had homemade leggings they wrapped around the bottom of their uniform legs to keep the lower part of the uniform legs clean and protected from thorns and briars. (See photo of the Kennedy Twins in their re-enacting uniforms. Ron is on the left as you look at the photo. I am wearing a uniform with leggings—also called gators).

Our old gray mule "ole Jeff" died one cold winter. Dad decided to buy a mare (female horse) that was for sale in a neighboring community. Ole Jeff had us spoiled. Plowing with ole Jeff was easy. He responded to verbal commands, gee (go to the right), haw (go to the left), whoa (stop), and git-up (move forward) with very little need to use the reins (we called reins *plow-lines*). The mare, whose name was Dolly, proved to be a challenge when it came to plowing. Donald and I were excited because she was a fine-looking riding mare. Unfortunately, she did not take well to the plowing harness. It took two people to plow with Dolly, one to control her with reins and the other to hold and steer the plow. Dad asked Uncle Frank to help "the boys" break the mare to the harness and plowing. Donald and I took turns "reining" her while Uncle Frank handled the plow—which required considerable skill to keep the plow point from digging too deep or too shallow and going straight. Late one afternoon, when we were almost finished plowing the five-acre field, Uncle Frank sent me up to the barn to get something. Donald had the plow lines in hand and was doing a good job controlling Dolly when I *headed off* to the barn. I heard a *commotion* down at the bottom of the field. I looked back, and all I could see was Dolly going in a full run with the plow bouncing behind her, Uncle Frank hollering and laughing for all he was worth, and Donald spinning in circles as fast as a child's top while holding both hands around his right leg about six inches above his knee. It seemed the plow turned over a large section of grass, which was the hiding place of a three-foot black snake (it was most likely a rat snake). The poor snake was rolled over by the plow, covered in dirt, and knew that he needed another safe place to hide. The first hiding place the poor feller (fellow) saw was Donald's trouser leg, and up he went! Yet another reason to wear leggings while plowing! Needless to say, Donald was not pleased with his new friend.

I laughed about that incident in the cornfield years later every time I buttoned my homemade leggings as I got ready to re-enact a *Civil War* battle with the 12th Louisiana Infantry CSA. We called the homemade

Mule drawn plows typical of the ones used by the Kennedy Twins. Plow in the foreground is a "middle-buster" the one behind and to right is a "harrow." (Photo taken at MS Ag Museum Jackson, MS).

leggings gators because the bottoms dragged along the ground like an alligator's belly while we marched. The gators were homemade leggings, and I proudly keep them. My sister-in-law (Donald's wife) made them. She made them from a copy of an original pattern, the material is a light canvas, and the buttons are wooden. Uncle Frank did not use leggings, but I do recall him occasionally wrapping the bottom of his trouser legs and also tying them with a cord. His habit of tying a cord around the bottom of his trouser legs not only kept dirt out of his brogans but prevented frightened snakes from going up the legs of his trousers. Trousers are not the correct term because Uncle Frank and the other farmers wore bib overalls, not trousers. Sadly, sometimes it is only years later when you realize just how smart the old folks really were. How I wish I had spent more time talking and listening to them.

Our forty-five-*acre* farm was originally a part of Grandfather Kennedy's initial forty-acre farm that he had expanded to some 120-*acres*. Donald and I never met our Kennedy grandparents—they died several years before we were born. Dad told us that after his mom and dad died, the farm was divided between our uncles and aunts. Aunt Minnie Bell, the oldest girl, Uncle Claude (1897-1958) the oldest boy and Uncle Ellis (1909-1994) all sold their portions and moved away. Aunt Minnie Bell sold her land after she got married. Uncles Ellis and Claude sold their land and moved away seeking employment opportunities. Dad, Uncle Lloyd, and Aunt Hattie all kept their parcels, built homes, and raised their families on the land originally settled by John Wesley Kennedy — who was a private in the 38th Mississippi Infantry, CSA, during the War.

Dad told us about how he, his father, and the other boys plowed the fields. He said they were always barefooted except during the coldest part of the winter. After a while, your feet toughen-up and nothing but the sharpest thorns would be a bother. He did say that one of the bad parts of plowing barefooted was that the plow would often turn up arrow heads. These projectile points, made by the Choctaw Indians, were very sharp. Before the white *plain folks* settled that part of Mississippi, the land had been Choctaw territory. The arrowheads were most likely left over or lost from Choctaw hunting parties. The number of lost arrowheads increased over generations of Indian occupation of the land. Dad said that they would cut their tough feet on those Indian arrowheads while plowing. The arrowheads had no value at that time. They simply picked them up and threw them over next to the fence where no one would step on them. Donald and I found many arrowheads on our land while growing-up, but we never kept them — just something else you never think about as a youth.

A Word About Brogans

Brogans were the work shoes worn by farmers and field hands. The word is derived from an Old Irish word "broc," which means shoe in the native Gallic language of the Irish. The Scotch and Irish were making and wearing brogans as early as the 1500s. Brogans were adopted and issued by the United States military soon after independence — many Revolutionary soldiers wore homemade brogans. Initially, the military issued shoes (brogans) were cheaper and easier to make than standard brogans because left and right were made the same — they were not shaped to fit the left or right foot. The shaping (breaking-in the shoe) occurred by the soldier's feet — which caused a lot of blistering! This was the standard military-issue footwear from the 1820s until shortly before the War for Southern Independence (1860s). The "blistering brogans" were replaced with more comfortable left/right brogans in the 1850s on orders of the United States Secretary of War. The Secretary of War, who replaced the blistering brogans with more comfortable brogans, was a Mexican American War hero, Jefferson Davis — later to become the President of the Confederate States of America!

Brogans used by Ron Kennedy as Re-enactor.

Chapter 15:

THE DINNER BELL
THE COMMUNITY'S 911 CALL

*Kennedy Dinner Bell used to call for help when
Great Uncle Charlie Kennedy's house caught fire.*

IN OUR MODERN SOCIETY, anytime there is an emergency, when you need the police, the fire department, or medical help, we can quickly summon help by dialing 911 on our phones. But *back in the day*, before cell phones, before land-line telephones, our rural Southern community had its own 911 system to call for help. It was the *dinner* bell.

Dad told us about what happened when his Uncle Charlie Kennedy's house caught on fire. Great Uncle Charlie Kennedy (1871-1948) was married to Great Aunt Vivian. Dad was a young boy, 10 or 12 years old at the time. On a clear summer day, he heard an unusual sound coming from Uncle Charlie's house, which was about half a mile down the road—to the east. When Dad looked in that direction, he saw smoke coming out of Uncle Charlie's house. He grabbed the pull cord on the *dinner* bell and began pulling it as fast as he could. His brother, Lloyd, grabbed the double-barreled shotgun and fired it in the air. Soon, every *dinner* bell in the community was ringing, and the men folk were headed toward the fire.

According to Dad and Uncle Lloyd, the community came together and helped Uncle Charlie and Aunt Vivian replace their house and furnish it with the basic necessities for family life. Aunt Vivian said that one of the things they saved from the fire was the family Bible. The family Bible was not only a valuable spiritual aid, but it also contained the records of births, marriages, and deaths of family members. Ladies of the community brought extra cloth and clothing; they provided even simple things such as needles, thread, and buttons. Mr. Ben Page fired up his saw-mill and Cousin Mike Guess provided logs for the framing of a new house. The children were taken in by family members until their new house was ready. It was a mutual effort of *kith and kin*, all brought together by an alarm announced by the *dinner* bell.

Dinner bells were rung slowly at noon time to tell the *field hands* it was time to come to *dinner*—remember, in the South, the noon meal is dinner, and the evening meal is *supper*. Each bell had its own distinctive tone. Dad and Mom said that you could tell whose *dinner* bell was ringing just by the sound it made. Anytime the bell is rung other than noon, and rung very fast, it was a sign of distress. Mom told us about how old folks who became ill and needed help rang the *dinner* bell to summon help. At that time, no electric lines were making humming noise, no cars or planes were creating noise, no radio or TV blasting music, and no air conditioners. It was a time of almost zero noise pollution. In such a quiet environment, sounds carried for long distances. When a bell began ringing at a fast rate, everyone within miles was able to hear it and understand that *something's the matter*. It was the Christian duty of all hearing the distress call to drop what they were doing and immediately answer the call for help. It was a part of our Southern tradition best described by a deacon in our local church, Mr. Polk Page, who always reminded us that it was our Christian duty to "help your fellow man." He believed it, and he lived it.

Southern historian, Frank Lawrence Owsley, in his 1949 book "Plain Folk of the Old South," described how the settlers of the South, while zealously individualistic, were also very community-centered. Christians have the duty to help one and another. This duty revealed itself as an attachment to the neighborly obligation to *kith and kin* (friends, neighbors, and/or relatives). This obligation to *kith and kin* was a principle that helped these early settlers survive. Except for a few large cities, most of the South's territory in 1860 could be classified as frontier. The C.S.A. was essentially a frontier nation struggling to maintain its freedom from an industrial empire.

The Southern tradition of obligation to *kith and kin* was crucial to survival on the frontier. Even by the time of *the War*, the South was still sparsely settled over most of its territory. Under such circumstances, people depended on their *kith and kin* when they needed help. This legacy of neighborly obligation was passed down to successive generations. As one Southern scholar wrote, "When the north went to war it went to war as an industrial empire—when the South went to war, it went to war as a family fighting to protect each other." One liberal democrat politician writing about how the South fought *the War* noted "The Northern army was most often run like a business, solving problems. The Southern army was run like a family, confronting a human crisis." Confederate General Pierre Gustave Toutant Beauregard of Louisiana said it best: "The Federal troops came as invaders, and the Southern troops stood as defenders of their homes, and further than this we need not go." It was not that different from the way Scottish Clans fought to protect their people from English invaders.

Frank Lawrence Owsley in "Plain Folk of the Old South" noted how neighbors took care of each other in times of crisis. There was no such thing as homeowners insurance to replace a house destroyed in a fire. If a house burned down, the community came together to help the family replace lost items and to rebuild the house. If a farmer in the neighborhood became bed-ridden due to illness or injury, the community took turns "plowing out his crops." (Dad and the rest of the community did this for Uncle Lloyd when his mule kicked him and broke his leg. William Faulkner wrote that, "a mule will work for you ten years for the privilege of kicking you once.") These *plain folks* were the non-plantation whites who made up the largest part of the South's white population. They would eventually make up the larger part of the Confederate Army. They referred to themselves as *plain folk*. They placed value on their culture that stressed spiritual values, whereas Yankees placed value on a culture that stressed materialistic values. From the very beginning of the United States there was a conflict between these two very different value systems; the Southern system was based on spiritual values whereas the Yankee system was based on material values—economics and the love of money. This resulted in most Yankee historians and writers describing the South's *plain folk* as being poor. In fact, most were *well off* with large herds of cattle and hogs roaming the South's vast open range. Free ranging livestock was a store of value roaming the South's back woods unseen to the casual

When Rebel Was Cool

Yankee observer who measured wealth and therefore value in money and the material things that money could buy.

This cultural conflict and inability of those schooled in the Yankee's materialistic culture to understand the South continues today. For example, the people living in the poorest state in the Union, Mississippi, today contribute far more per capita to charity than the people living in one of the richest states, Massachusetts. The 2019 per capita income in Mississippi was $37,994. Mississippi, out of her relative poverty, answered the spiritual call to help your fellow man. The 2019 per capita income of Massachusetts was $70,073. Massachusetts, out of her wealth, stingily held on to her material wealth and left it to the government to help their fellow man. This demonstrates why Southern historian Grady McWhiney wrote that the War for Southern Independence was not a war over slavery; it was a war of culture against culture. But the victor writes and enforces his version of the war, and uses his political and social power to exclude, limit, and in effect censor knowledge about the invaded peoples' side of the story. Therefore, most Southerners will never know the truth about their ancestors struggle to establish a government based upon the free and unfettered consent of the governed. A right that was boldly proclaimed by the Thirteen American Colonies in 1776 in their Joint Declaration of Independence and symbolized by the Liberty Bell.

The Liberty Bell, symbolizing the American principle that, "Governments are instituted among Men, deriving their just powers from the consent of the governed. That whenever any Form of Government becomes destructive of these ends, it is the Right of the People to alter or to abolish it, and to institute new Government," as per the American Declaration of Independence. If it was true in 1776, then it was also true in 1861. Both King George, III in 1776 and Abraham Lincoln in 1861 knew that the only alternative to secession is coercion. Coercion and "consent of the governed" cannot coexist! Consent represents freedom – coercion represents tyranny.
(Photo from: "https://www.nps.gov/inde/learn/historyculture/stories-libertybell.htm")

Chapter 16:

THE OLE SWIMMING HOLE DAYS BEFORE SWIMMING POOLS

The community swimming hole. (Artwork Charles Hayes).

MANY, IF NOT MOST, public schools in the South today have swim teams as part of their athletic department. When the average young Southerners today think about going swimming, they think about a local public or private swimming pool. But *back in the day* in the rural South, we had no access to such "citified novelties." When we wanted to go swimming, we had to decide which "swimming hole" to use— meaning which creek, river, or lake. The girls, being fashion-minded, all had store-bought swimsuits, but many of the boys wore cut-off blue jeans. By the time we were old enough to go to high school, the boys had store-bought swimming trunks—mainly because we wanted to impress the girls.

Donald and I learned to swim when we were ten or eleven years old. A few of us boys from the church got together and went down to Peggy Creek in an area where we were baptized. The place was not large enough to do much swimming, so we collected about ten *croaker sacks* from the barn, took them to the creek, filled them with sand, and dammed up the creek. Our dam created a small but very handy swimming hole—at least until the next rain came and washed away our *croaker sack*, sandbag dam.

Only one of the boys, Tony Douglas (1949-1991) Brother Douglas' oldest son, knew how to swim. But most of the swimming hole was not over shoulder deep. Several of the adults had told us that they had learned to swim by making "water wings" out of gourds tied in *croaker sacks*. The novice swimmer pushed a gourd to each side of the sack and lay between the gourds. This gave him enough floatation to keep his head above the water while he practiced kicking and arm strokes—arm strokes for the novice consisted of what we called "dog paddling" because it resembled the way dogs swim. At some point, the other boys removed the water-wings, and off the new swimmer went! No adults, no lifeguards, no goggles, no safety equipment, and water in which it was impossible to see your feet—just a bunch of *good ole boys* having fun in the creek.

We did not have any gourds to use for making water-wings. You have to harvest the gourds in the summer and allow them to dry over the winter. We did not think that far ahead! We substituted molasses cans for gourds. The cans were the size of a gallon paint can. We

Syrup mill, mule, horse, or ox pulls cane press, juice flows or carried to cooker in background. (Photo LOC).

The Ole Swimming Hole

cleaned the empty cans and securely replaced the lids to make them water tight. Two molasse cans and one *croaker sack* with the open end of the sack tied off was all we needed.

Mr. Emery Page was busy plowing his field about 50 yards from where we were playing and taking turns practicing with our water-wings. He stopped his plowing and came over to see what we were doing. Mr. Page took off his brogans (shoes), and got down in the creek with us. He grabbed one of us by our belt loop, holding us up while we kicked and dog paddled around the swimming hole. He slowly eased up on the belt loop until we were swimming on our own. He must have spent an hour or more helping to teach us how to swim.

Mr. Emery Page was not related to any of us boys at the swimming hole. But he was part of our community, we knew him, saw him every Sunday at church, and we played and went to school with his children. He was part of our *kith and kin*. The fact that an adult stopped his work and took the time to teach us to swim did not seem unusual to us at the time. Looking back, I can see just how important community and church were to those of us lucky enough to grow up in what most modern folks would consider an impoverished South. Materially, by the world's criteria, we were poor, but spiritually, we were rich and blessed.

We graduated to a much better swimming hole once we became teenagers and started riding horses. Mr. George Page, who lived further down Peggy Creek not far from where it ran into the Pearl River, had a great swimming hole on his land. With his permission, the young folks got together and cut a trail through the woods to the swimming hole. We had a diving board and a large rope tied to a tree on the creek bank. We used the rope to swing out over the swimming hole and drop into the cold water. The swimming hole also had a small sand bar the girls used as a sunbathing area. On many a hot summer day, we often ended our horse riding at that swimming hole. It was also a gathering place for teenagers after Sunday church during the summer. Every community had a creek, lake, or river "swimming hole," and by the end of the summer, we spent time swimming in each. The best memories of my life are riding horses and swimming in Mr. George's swimming hole. Mr. George was a deacon in our local Baptist Church. He also had a syrup mill that each fall was used to process our sugar cane into molasses. His wife and our mother were great friends. We were a community—we were *kith and kin*. It was often jokingly said that our community, Pearl Valley, was "Page town, Guess street, Kennedy hotel, and nothing to eat." We were blessed to have grown-up when giants walked among us disguised as poor Southern farmers.

Tony Douglas (1948-1991) Vietnam Veteran.

A Note About Tony Douglas — Brother Douglas' Eldest Son

Tony graduated from high school in 1968 at the height of the Vietnam War. Being a patriotic young man and following his father's proud legacy of military service, Tony joined the U. S. Marines. After basic training he was sent to Vietnam. While in Vietnam he was assigned the duty of mixing a special defoliant called Agent Orange. Although he survived the Vietnam War, he did not survive Agent Orange. In early 1990 he suffered an illness the origin of which physicians could not explain. Tony died in 1991, he was 43 years old. The United States government refused to admit any culpability regarding Tony's "unusual," post-Vietnam, illness, and death. We should always support our troops but the government's bureaucrats and politicians — that is another matter altogether! Rest in peace friend of my youth. He taught us to swim in Peggy Creek, and then, crossed the Jordan River ahead of us all.

Chapter 17:

MOVING A TOWN ON OX WAGONS

THE ONLY GRANDPARENTS Donald and I knew were Grandfather and Grandmother Berry. Dad's parents died years before we were born. I think I have some memory of once seeing Grandfather Theodore Kennedy's brother, Great Uncle Charlie Kennedy, who was married to Great Aunt Vivian. But the only grandparents we knew were on Mom's side of the family. Donald and I spent a lot of time "a visiting" or talking to Granddaddy Berry. He was full of family history on Mom's side of the family.

Our Berry grandparents owned a fair amount of farmland in the late 1920s. Out of necessity, farmers, just before planting season, borrowed enough money from local banks to purchase seed, fertilizer, and other necessities required to *make a crop*. Remember, the South was cash poor since *the War*, which did not improve much until well after World War II. *Back in the day*, Southern farmers were especially sensitive to market fluctuations of cotton prices, which was their primary cash crop. The times when the market price of cotton was high were known as "good times." In good times, the family made enough money on their cotton crop to pay off the bank loan with cash left over to see them through the winter and maybe a little extra disposable income. A Southern farmer seldom made enough money to create cash "savings." Economist refer to this as "capital accumulation." No people can lift themselves out of poverty without savings and the resulting investments (capital accumulation). Without the ability to build up capital savings, Southern farmers were forced to remain in the cruel cycle of borrowing, planting, paying off the bank, making it through the winter and beginning the cycle again next spring. It was essential to pay off (repay the loan) the bank first because it held a mortgage on or a lien against the farmer's land and home. In hard times, when the price of cotton was low, it was hard for some to repay the bank. If the farmer failed to pay off the mortgage, the bank foreclosed and the family lost their land and home. When this happened, the only option for most was to become homeless sharecroppers—a new form of slavery, according to many scholars, as well as religious and political leaders who lived at the time and were actual witnesses to sharecropping. At its peak sharecropping bound over 8 million Southerners—at least 60% were white Southerners. One scholar noted that while farmers outside of the South were advancing into modern, scientific, mechanized farming—Southern farmers were stuck in 19th century farming methods. This was not by choice. It was of necessity created by poverty imposed upon the Southern people by the victors in the War for Southern Independence. The Kennedy Twins outline this in "Punished With Poverty-the Suffering South" and "Yankee Empire: Aggressive Abroad and Despotic at Home."

Granddaddy Berry told us that when he and his identical twin brother were small boys, they took every opportunity to go to Rockport. At that time, Rockport sat on the banks of the Pearl River. He said that he (Walt) and his twin brother (Willie) raced barefooted down the dirt road in Rockport when they heard a steam boat coming up river, blowing its steam whistle. It did not seem strange to me that he said that they would race barefooted. Shoes were at a premium in

Twins Walter and Willie Berry
— the Kennedy Twins' Grandfather and Great Uncle. Photo circa 1900.

the impoverished South. A situation that did not radically improve until well after World War II. *Field hands* usually had *brogans*, but the young children and many of the women went barefooted. Children going barefooted was common up to the late 1950s but it was not a choice; it was a necessity in the intentionally impoverished South.

Hookworm was one of the many diseases that tormented the rural South since the end of *the War*. The parasite was not a major problem before *the War*, but after *the War*, with the destruction of the South's infrastructure and Northern imposed poverty, hookworm and other diseases became major health issues. Hookworm ravaged the post-War South, but, to *add insult to injury*, the Northern imposed poverty that created the situation promoting the spread of the disease was ignored by the powers that be in Washington, D.C. The hookworm infection rate in Mississippi in 1915 was 34% for adults and 37% for children. The South's warm, humid climate, and sandy loam soil allows the hookworm parasite to remain dormant in the soil. When a barefoot comes in contact with the parasite in the soil, the parasite will quickly bore its way corkscrew-like into the bare skin. It has been estimated by one scholar that, post-War, hookworm caused a million deaths in the South. Such Southern suffering, disease, and death could have been avoided had the conquered, occupied and impoverished South been treated with the same leniency, tolerance, and charity that the United States treated the defeated and occupied people of Germany and Japan post World War II. But such was not the case.

Rockport is no longer on the Pearl River. Granddaddy Berry told us that when the G M & O (Gulf Mobile and Ohio) railroad came through, all the stores down on the river closed. The railroad was much more efficient than steamboats on small rivers such as the Pearl River. Some of the stores were jacked-up and put on frames with logging wagon-wheels attached to the frames and pulled by yokes of oxen to the new Rockport next to the railroad depot. It required moving these buildings about two miles over dirt roads. The new Rockport was located west of the old Rockport river landing. Granddaddy said you could hear the cracking of bullwhips for miles around as the *drovers* guided the yokes of oxen from the river to the railroad crossing. Years later, when Donald and I were in the second grade at the Rockport elementary school, which had only three classrooms, the teacher took the first and second-grade classes for picnics down to the old port on the river. I still remember seeing the piers that were left where the steamboats tied up in years gone by. Can you imagine today a second-grade teacher, by herself, taking 20 or so students on a picnic on a river bank?

The ground-seal (mud-seal) used for smokehouse construction

Above is an example of a smokehouse with ground-seal placed directly on ground. The ground-seal, also called a mud seal, is a pine log with high rosin content that prevents (limits) rotting. The space between the logs was sealed with a red clay and straw mixture making it air tight (taut). The Kennedy family's smokehouse had a similar ground-seal but the walls were made of rough-cut sap-wood board-and-batting instead of logs. (Photo from MS AG Museum Jackson, MS).

Chapter 18:

TV COMES TO THE RURAL SOUTH

Early Radio (left) with large dial and early TV (right) with small screen. (Photographs authors personal collection).

RURAL ELECTRIFICATION was a big deal for the South in the early 1950s. By that time, the emerging electric power grid connected the cities and towns. But electricity came to the rural South very slowly. While electrical power companies could make profits in cities, it was a different story in rural areas. Electrical wire was strung long distances in rural areas, requiring the setting of many poles. The demand for electric power in rural areas was less than in the cities. The primary reason most farmers wanted electricity was to power lights in their homes. Early on, rural Southerners used electricity to power one or two light bulbs hanging from the ceiling. The switch to turn the bulb off and on was a simple pull string attached to a switch on the socket into which the bulb was screwed. For many years, "light poles" was the common term used to refer to the poles holding up the electric wire running along rural roads. Other electric conveniences added were fans, either window fans that pulled air through windows throughout the house or oscillating fans placed in one room, a radio, and eventually a refrigerator. It was in the mid to late 1960s before telephone lines were run throughout the rural South.

When Rebel Was Cool

I recall the first time I saw a TV set. It was 1951, and we were in New Orleans, Louisiana, visiting Dad's brother, our Uncle Ellis. Mom pointed to it and asked if we knew what it was. Donald and I were four years old at the time. We both said it was a radio. We thought it was a radio because it was not turned on, and the TV screen looked very similar to the large dial on many radios of the time. In 1955, Mom and Dad purchased our first television set. Our cousin, Shelby Guess, was the first person in the community to acquire a TV set. A lot of folks went to his house on Friday nights to watch the Grand Ole Opry. It became sort of a contest to see how fast each family could obtain a TV set. You could tell which families had a TV because the reception of the weak signal required a tall antenna on top of the house. In our part of Mississippi, we had only two TV stations to select from, and those stations broadcast only at certain times of the day and night. They came on at 6 AM and went off the air at midnight. One of the last things the station did before going off the air was to play the national anthem. Radio stations often played *Dixie* at the beginning of their broadcast day and the national anthem at the end of their broadcast day. When the TV stations were not on the air, their signal consisted of a test pattern that was broadcast continuously during "off the air" hours.

Before we got our first TV set, Mom listened to day time soap operas broadcast on radio. Radio and eventually TV programs called soap operas got that title because the primary advertisers were companies that sold laundry detergents. This was because the audience for these day time programs were stay-at-home-moms (who were the vast majority of moms back in the day). Radio programs similar to "The Secret Storm," "As the World Turns," and "The Guiding Light" made the transition from day time radio soap operas to TV daytime soap operas. Many of the stay-at-home moms kept up with soap operas via radio and later via TV while ironing clothes and doing other house work. Before we had a TV, our older brother, Alton (1938-2018), listened to radio programs at night. Three programs I recall him listening to were cowboy programs "Gene Audrey," "The Lone Ranger," and "Roy Rogers." I still recall the opening words of his favorite radio program. It was not a cowboy program. It was a crime-thriller series called "The Shadow." At the beginning of each radio program, the announcer asked "Who knows what evil lurks in the hearts of men? The Shadow knows!" The Shadow was a crime fighting vigilante. It had a good following, but I don't think it made it to TV.

Before Mom and Dad built their new house, they lived in the house Dad inherited when Grandmother Kennedy passed away. Dad's father built it and it was the house in which he and his brothers and sisters grew up. Of course, it was built long before rural electrification—most likely, it was built in the late 1890s. But even though Mom and Dad did not have electricity via a yet to be established power grid, they still had a radio in the old house. Mom and Dad purchased a small, inexpensive, secondhand, generator. It produced enough electricity to power an old vacuum tube radio. Vacuum tube radios generated a fair amount of heat—which caused the tubes to eventually "burn out." It took up to 30 seconds after you turned the radio on for the tubes to "warm-up." After the radio "warmed up," it would then begin to play.

Transistors eventually replaced vacuum tubes. William Shockley invented transistors in 1947, but it took a couple of decades before they became standard in electronic equipment such as radios and TV sets. Transistors do the same thing as the vacuum tubes, but they do it with less power requirement, less heat production, and transistors take up much less space than vacuum tubes. Transistors made the development of microprocessors possible and are the key elements required for the development of computers and all the electronic communication, household, and other devices that have become an integral part of our daily lives.

Getting a source of electricity for the radio in the old house was just part of the challenge. The radio signal coming from Jackson, Mississippi at the time was not very strong. In addition to a weak signal, Jackson was about 50 miles away—*as the crow flies*. To capture enough of the weak signal, Dad strung a thin wire on top of the house running across the entire length of the roof at its highest point. A lot of folks refused to do this because of the fear that it would attract lightning. To protect the house, Dad installed lightning rods that were higher than the radio antenna. He connected the lightning rods to a copper rod that he sank several feet into the ground. A similar precaution was done for the TV antenna when we got our first TV. The TV antenna was situated on top of the house. Dad connected the metal pole to the grounding cable and connected the grounding cable to the grounding rod driven into the ground. Within a few years, the TV signals coming from the Jackson TV stations were strong enough that Dad was able to remove the antenna from the top of the house and placed the antenna's pole on the ground next to the house.

Donald and I lived when the rural South was trying to catch up with the rest of the nation. The rural South became electrified; many of the dusty gravel roads were paved; and we experienced the arrival of TV and telephones. While telephones came to the community when we were still in grade school, Mom and Dad could not afford a phone until we were grown and on our own. We lived in a time when poverty was slowly being pushed back—at least relative to the poverty experienced by prior generations of Southern *kith and kin*.

When Rebel Was Cool

Relative to the rest of the United States, the South in the 1950s and early 1960s still lagged well behind the rest of the United States—just as it does even today.

I recall seeing steam locomotives going through Hazlehurst on the Illinois Central Railroad and others going through Rockport and Oma on the Gulf Mobile and Ohio Railroad (G M & O). Great clouds of black smoke and gushing steam filled the air. The train's steam whistle and its clanging bell announced its arrival. Steam locomotives were divided into those that carried freight and those that carried passengers. It was a sign of the changing times when steam locomotives were gradually replaced with new, modern Diesel locomotives, and this change became more rapid after the end of World War II (1945). In the 1950s Dad often took a train to his welding job in New Orleans. He left on Monday morning and returned Friday night. Dad rode to his welding job in New Orleans on the first Diesel passenger train that ran in Mississippi. It ran on the G M & O track that came through Rockport and Oma on the way to New Orleans. The train was named "The Rebel." Other fanciful names of locomotives included one called "The Dixie Flyer." Mom took Dad to the train depot at Oma early on Monday morning. We waited there to watch him get on board. I can still hear young black boys yelling as the train approached "Here comes de Rebel, here comes de Rebel." It was a beautiful sight for those of us who were used to seeing steam locomotives. Years later in high school at Wesson, we watched as the "Panama Limited" and the "City of New Orleans" flew past the

Uncle Ellis and Dad circa 1909

TV Comes to the Rural South

G M & O's "The Rebel" at Bogalusa, LA 9-17-1953.
About the time Dad would have rode "The Rebel" to New Orleans.
Photo by William H. B. Jones. (Photo courtesy of David Price).

The Kennedy Twins' home, built by our Dad in 1946
a year before we were born. Photo taken in 1946.

Chapter 19:

STARVATION — THE HUNGRY SOUTH

WE WERE NEVER HUNGRY; no one we knew ever suffered from lack of food. We ate a lot of corn bread and vegetables that were grown in our garden. Meat was eaten once a week, on Sunday, and then it was a home-raised chicken or home-grown pork. When Mom and Dad talked about hard times during the Great Depression 1929-41, they always said that while each one of their families (Kennedy and Berry) never had much in the way of money, they never went hungry. This was a major advantage of being a rural society — if you owned your own land, you could always grow your food. Mom said, "Our food may not have been the best, but our stomachs were never empty." Even though Mom's family was technically sharecroppers, they were *better off* than most sharecroppers because they were sharecropping on land owned by Grandmother Berry's brother, Great Uncle George Little (1899-1972). He owned many acres and had a successful saw mill. Unlike most sharecroppers, once our Berry grandparents began sharecropping for Uncle George, they did not move from place to place each planting season. Unlike most other "croppers" they were never in danger of being evicted from tenant houses.

Today, very few people in the South, if any, spend time worrying about their next meal. But even in my days as a young person in the rural South, the memory of hunger still bore heavily on the old folks if only at a subconscious level. Today, it is difficult for the younger generation to understand the impact the memory of hunger had on the mind-set of Southerners well after *the War*. Because today's generation of Southerners are taught "history" out of Yankee-authored textbooks and are instructed by teachers educated in the South's postmodern, left-of-center, neo-Marxist Universities — they have no understanding of the South's true history. This lack of understanding is very convenient for the victor—it provides the invader with justification for his aggressive invasion, and it helps him maintain political control of the conquered South.

Hunger and malnutrition were unheard of in the South before *the War*, but during and after *the War*, it was a universal concern. Yankee history "scholars" carefully avoid this topic and cover-up their nation's criminal abuses by endlessly claiming the South was trying to maintain slavery, and therefore, we deserved the punishment we got. But the truth that Yankee "scholars" prefer that you never know is that poverty and starvation were intentionally inflicted upon the people of the South by the United States of America. They used starvation during *the War* as a war measure—an act held to be illegal by international standards (a war crime)—and they inflicted starvation on the South post-War as part of our punishment for attempting to leave their Union.

Starvation of the Southern civilian population was one of the North's war strategies. Such war strategies directed against the civilian population violated international rules of civilized warfare. These international rules of warfare were acknowledged and accepted by all civilized nations of the day. But empires only follow the rules of civilized warfare when it is to the empire's advantage. All across the South, invading Yankee armies deliberately destroyed not only existing civilian food (and medical) supplies, but they also destroyed the farm implements, animals, and fences necessary for future food production. They did this to create mass starvation. Their aim was to prevent Southerners from planting and growing crops the following year. Confederate President Jefferson Davis was forced to recommend the eating of rats as a means to avoid mass starvation of the South's civilian population. But things did not improve after the South surrendered. Malnutrition became a major problem for the post-War South thanks to the new form of slavery, sharecropping, which entrapped a large percentage of white and black Southerners for almost a century after *the War*.

The United States' invasion, conquest, occupation, and exploitation of the South vividly demonstrate the truth of the saying, "Empires do not invade a free people to improve the lot of the people in the invaded, conquered, and occupied nation." The ability of a people to feed themselves is key to their survival. A study of Southern food production before and after *the War* demonstrated the radical decline in the ability of Southerners to feed themselves post-War. Six Southern counties were studied, three in Mississippi and three in Alabama. Before *the War*, these counties were food exporters—they grew enough food to feed themselves and export the excess. In 1930, almost 65 years after *the War*, these counties were food importers—

they did not produce enough food to feed themselves. Before *the War*, hog production equaled 2.1 hogs per person, but 65 years after the North's glorious victory, hog production dropped to 0.4 per person. Hog meat was a primary source of protein in the Southern diet. Loss of this source of protein led to the South-only disease of *pellagra*. Corn production before *the War* was 48.5 bushels per person, but 65 years later, it had fallen to 22.8 bushels per person. What had happened? Before *the War*, the farms in these counties were privately own—many of them being small farms individually owned by families belonging to what we call the *plain folk* of the old South. After *the War*, 71% of the farms operated under the system of sharecropping—a system that, in many respects, was worse than slavery. Donald and I go into great detail discussing the South's intentional impoverishment in "Punished With Poverty-the Suffering South."

Sharecropping—post-War slavery. Photo taken circa 1940 in New Madrid County, Missouri, (Photo LOC).

An elderly friend in North Louisiana told us about his grandmother who declared "They tried to starve us to death after *the War*." This was from someone who lived in an area of the South that had not been visited by massive Yankee armies, yet such was the destruction visited upon the South that starvation was common everywhere.

The sharecropper's poor diet produced mass malnutrition across the post-War South. But looking at the diet of *antebellum* (pre-War) slaves, we find their diet was much better than post-War white and black sharecroppers' diet! A Nobel Laureate in Economic Science noted that the slave's diet "exceeded modern (1964) recommended daily levels of the chief nutrients." What does this say about the North that continually brags about how they made war on the South in the name of freedom? In fact, the Yankee victors intentionally impoverished both black and white Southerners. The South became an economic and political colony of the prosperous and powerful North. Post-War Southerners became second-class people in an otherwise prosperous United States of America. This impoverishment created massive malnutrition which weakened the physical bodies of many Southerners and made them susceptible to diseases that were either unheard of or at least well-controlled before *the War*. *Vae Victus*—woe to the vanquished, the unofficial motto of all empires.

A Word About Sharecropping— 8.5 Million and 60% Were White

As noted, our maternal grandparents were sharecroppers. The system of sharecropping was adopted by black and white Southerners after *the War* because it was the only way many Southerners could afford to "raise a crop." It cost money to buy seed, fertilizer, plow animals, feed for animals, provide food and shelter for the animals, and the family while you are waiting for fall harvest. There was almost no money left in the South after the Yankees came through. So landowners would borrow money from Northern controlled banks at a very high interest rate and use that money to *grub stake* landless black and white families who would farm the land owner's land. At harvest time the sharecropper keeps between 40 to 50% of the money received from the harvest, repay the landowner the money advanced at planting time, and hopefully have enough left over to survive during the coming winter.

Sharecropping ended by 1965-7. Donald and I went to school with the children of two sharecropping families. They were good people, but poor by the world's standards. All the children in the sharecropping families we knew became successful in their chosen occupations. Bishop Anthony Durier of Louisiana in his Pastoral Letter of March 2, 1899, wrote that sharecropping was "a new form of slavery." Senator James Eastland of Mississippi, in a 1940s speech, declared sharecropping to be a form of slavery that the United States intentionally ignores. *Vae Victus*—Woe to the vanquished. The actual or unacknowledged motto of all empires!

Starvation

Two families of evicted, homeless, sharecroppers, Missouri, circa 1930. (Photos courtesy Library of Congress).

Chapter 20:

SICKNESS AND DISEASE IN THE SOUTH

HEALTHCARE IS A TOPIC that modern-day politicians and social justice warriors enjoy talking about. *Back in the day*, there was very little concern about the health of rural Southerners even after World War II. In the early 1950s, there were very few hospitals serving rural areas of the South. Most births were home births with a local "midwife" in attendance. By that time (the early 1950s), most counties had physicians available at least in the county seat. But it had been a long and arduous struggle to overcome the diseases that afflicted the postWar South. One particular disease became known as a "South only" disease — a disease caused by malnutrition called *pellagra*.

The fact that history is real to Southerners was driven home to us when Donald and I discovered a document from a physician in Hazlehurst, Mississippi (the county seat of the county in which we were born), who was treating a woman in 1947 for *pellagra*. The document was written 82 years after *the War*! This woman was Grandfather Berry's sister-in-law — our great aunt! Honest Southern scholars and writers pointed out that *pellagra* was unheard of in the pre-War South, it was unheard of even during *the War*, but it became common across the South after Yankee victory and occupation of the South. For those Southerners who know their family history — *the past is never dead; it is not even past*. It is family, and it is part of our family's heritage of struggle that must not be forgotten. Our *people* have endured the sufferings of Job, and like Job, we have persevered, we have maintained our faith in the goodness of God, we have rejected the tyranny of evil, and we look forward to ultimate victory in this world or the next.

When Rebel Was Cool

Arkansas sharecropper's child suffering from malnutrition. (Photo LOC).

A Federal government document published in 1938 took note that, "The scourge of *pellagra*, that affects the South almost exclusively." This South-only disease lasted for almost a century, devastating over 3,000,000 Southerners and killing at least 100,000 people. The cure for this devastating disease was simple—improved diet, especially additional protein from meat consumption. The calloused indifference of the Federal government toward Southerners suffering from this South-only disease is demonstrated by the fact that during the Great Depression, to increase pork prices, the government slaughtered hogs by the thousands. The only folks to benefit from this effort to increase pork prices were the meat packing houses in Chicago. No thought was given to providing the meat to those suffering from *pellagra*. Today, very few in the medical profession even know what *pellagra* is, and they certainly do not know that it was virtually a South-only disease inflicted upon Southerners by the victors in the War for Southern Independence.

Hookworm, rickets, and malaria were diseases that also ravaged the post-War South up to the mid-1960s. Take a look at the photo of the white Arkansas sharecropper's young son. Notice that he is barefooted. Hookworm is a parasite that bores into the skin of bare feet. Going barefoot in an area where unsanitary, outdoor, toilets are common and where animal droppings are on the ground is a major cause for the transmission of the disease. Also, note the boy's bowed legs and distended stomach. It is a sign of rickets. A disease caused by malnutrition resulting in a deficiency of vitamin D. The photograph of the young black child leaning out a torn window screen is evidence, for those who know what to look for, of the transmission of malaria. Infected mosquitoes transmit malaria. The primary way to protect family members from mosquitoes is to have screen wire over all windows. But because sharecroppers did not own the houses lived in, they had little desire to make improvements — even if they had the disposable income necessary, which most did not. The land owner had little incentive to spend money on his sharecropper (tenant) houses because he was operating on a minimal margin (profit), and even when he made improvements, the tenants had little incentive to take care of the repairs because they most likely would not be living in that house the next planting season. This cycle of grinding poverty is typical for people who suffer invasion, conquest, and occupation. It is the result of the *cultural distortion* that occurs when a people are ruled by outside forces that do not understand the local society — rulers who hold the ruled people in contempt. *Cultural distortion* caused by an invader is a fact of history. Northerners may ignore this sad fact of our history, but Southerners have lived it. And it is not over because today we the people of *Dixie*, per capita the poorest section of America, are still living it!

Landless Southerners did not freely choose to become sharecroppers; landowners did not freely choose to become seemingly uncaring landlords; Southern political leaders did not freely choose to become a part of a *supreme federal government* (empire) — it was the only means available to *keep soul and body together*. In reality, as a conquered people, we had little choice. It was the only way to survive for millions after our society was suddenly and violently destroyed. The post-War Southern society is a result of a violent and relatively sudden revolution. It was not and is not the natural result of gradual evolution (change or growth) of Southern society — a society that, if not for Yankee invasion, would have slowly transformed itself into a better, freer, and prosperous society enjoyed by all its citizens. The opportunity for a natural evolution into

Tennant house for Texas sharecropper. Houses with no proper screen windows to keep mosquitoes out was a major factor in the spread of malaria. (Photo LOC).

a better society was denied the South at the point of bloody Yankee bayonets. Never forget whose blood is on those Yankee bayonets.

It was not until the early 1950s that health care in the South, and therefore, the general health of many Southerners, began to catch up with the rest of the United States. For a long time after *the War* and up to the 1950s, the health condition of many Southerners, especially those trapped in sharecropping, was far worse than it was for Southerners in the days before *the War*. One scholar noted that hookworm infection claimed one million lives in the postWar South. Scholars studying the conditions of slaves before *the War* as compared to the condition of black sharecroppers well after *the War* found the health of black Southerners deteriorated after *the War*. They noted that black sharecroppers' diets in the 1890s were protein and vitamin starved. Note that the same could have been said for white sharecroppers, but whites were not the subject of the study. The study noted that sickness rates among black sharecroppers were 20% higher than it was on plantations under slavery. This is pointed out not as an effort to justify slavery but to demonstrate how cruel the victorious Yankees treated all Southerners, black and white, after their glorious victory. Glory, Glory, Hallelujah — as in the "Battle Hymn of the Republic." Why is that Yankee Battle Hymn, written by a non-Christian, sung in our churches?

One of the cruelest chapters in the history of the North's callous use and abuse of black Southerners occurred shortly after the end of *the War*. In 1866, a smallpox epidemic broke out among freed slaves — then referred to as freedmen. The Federal government knew how to limit the spread of the disease via vaccinations and quarantine measures. But the Federal government did almost nothing to limit the spread of this terrible death-producing disease among the newly freed slaves. A black physician, Alexander T. Augusta, who was employed by the Federal government at that time, noted that the disease was spreading throughout the black population due to the failure of the Federal authorities to supply medical resources. Also, the unhealthy condition in which the freed slaves were forced to live since the destruction of the plantation system added to the spread of disease. Recall that when Lincoln was asked what would happen to the slaves after the plantation system was destroyed, he flippantly replied, "*root hog or die.*" As bad as their refusal to provide medical aid was the logic used by many in the Federal government to justify their reluctance to provide sufficient aid to the newly freed slaves was far worse — it was immoral.

Many of the Federal officials then in control were adherents to the *extinction theory*. The *extinction theory* held that black Southerners would soon die off and go extinct once the paternal protection provided by

Sickness and Disease in the South

the plantation system was destroyed. Therefore, those in authority in the Federal government thought that it would be a waste of resources to send aid to people who they thought would eventually die off — become extinct. Others in the Federal government took an aloof and indifferent attitude toward the harsh conditions that all Southerners, black and white, were suffering under.

A Yankee abolitionist and correspondent for the "Atlantic Monthly" demonstrated the general public's attitude, in the North, toward black Southerners when he wrote, "We say the Free States (Yankee states) should say, confine the Negro to the smallest possible area. Hem him in. Coop him up. Slough him off. Preserve just so much of North America as is possible for the white man." Yet, Yankee history "scholars" and Yankee authored text books slander the South as the seat of racism and hatred, while the South as a conquered nation has no adequate means to respond and defend its honor.

While many modern folks will deny that American political, military, and social leaders would endorse the extinction of an entire people, it is none-the-less, an inconvenient fact of American history. But it was not just black Southerners that Yankee leaders wanted to exterminate. They held the same opinion about white Southerners. Donald and I discuss this inhuman but well-hidden part of Yankee history in "Punished With Poverty-the Suffering South," and "Yankee Empire: Aggressive Abroad and Despotic at Home."

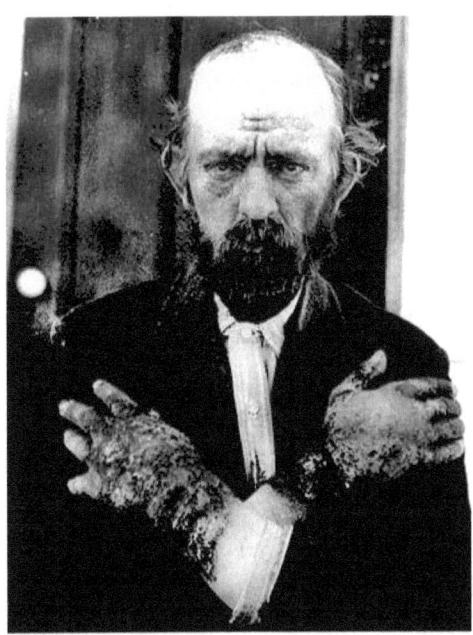

Pellagra was a South-only disease caused by post-War malnutrition.
A man suffering from pellagra. (Photo Library of Congress-LOC). Over three million Southerners suffered — over 100,000 died while the U.S.A did little to alleviate the starvation its invasion and conquest inflicted upon the Southern people. As the Communist dictator Joseph Stalin callously declared, "One death is a tragedy, a million is a statistic." Vae Vectus — woe to the vanquished! The unofficial motto of all empires.

Chapter 21

PHOTOS

First National Confederate Flag – also known as the Stars and Bars. On the battle field it looked too much like the U.S. Flag. A second flag was designed.

The Second National Flag of the Confederate States of America. It appears on the Confederate $500.00 bill. When the wind was not blowing it looked too much like a white surrender flag. A red bar was added to create the Third National Flag.

Third National Confederate Flag. The final and official flag of the Confederate States of America. Our national flag!

When Rebel Was Cool

The Confederate Battle Flag. Often labeled as the Rebel Flag. The first Rebel Flag is the Betsy Ross Thirteen-star Flag used by George Washington. The Confederate Battle Flag was never used as a national flag but was used by various Confederate Armies as a Battle Flag.

The Bonnie Blue Flag. First used as the flag of the Republic of West Florida (1812) when the parishes and counties of West Florida seceded from Spain. It was made popular by a song – "The Bonnie Blue Flag" – sung at the state capitol after Mississippi seceded from the United States. While widely used and adopted into many other flags, it was never an official flag.

The Republic of Mississippi Flag. Mississippi was a Sovereign Republic after it seceded from the United States and before it joined the Confederate States of America. The tree on the white field is a representation of a magnolia tree – the state tree of Mississippi. (Many other Southern States adopted Republic flags before they joined the Confederate States of America).

The Republic of Louisiana Flag. It flew over the State Capital in Baton Rouge after Louisiana seceded from the United States and before it joined the Confederate States of America. The flag reflects Louisiana's unique European heritage. The blue, white, and red stripes represent the tri-colors of the French Flag while the orange and yellow represent the colors of the Royal Spanish Flag, and the number of stripes, thirteen, represent the original Thirteen American Colonies that seceded from the British Empire in 1776.

Texas was an independent, sovereign, nation before it voluntarily joined the Union. Its state flag was carried in the War by many Texas units. Texas and Hawaii state flags are the only two state flags currently being used as state flags that also served as national flags before they were made a part of the United States.

H. K. Edgerton at gravesite of Black Confederate veteran Levi Carnine CSA.

Dr. Lenard Hynes, Sr. and Ron Kennedy circa 1992. Dr. Hynes addressed the LA Division of the Sons of Confederate Veterans, Ron was Division Commander.

Photos

Cotton Bowl 1960 LSU vs. Ole Miss Photo from Facebook posting.

President Jefferson Davis, C.S.A. used on cover of Was Jefferson Davis Right? Artist, Aubrey Hayden, original part of author's collection.

Painting by Jerry McWilliams, used on cover of Uncle Seth Fought the Yankees. *Original part of author's collection, now on loan to Beauvoir, The Jefferson Davis Home Biloxi, Mississippi.*

Painting by Stephanie Ford, used on cover of Dixie Rising-Rules for Rebels. *Original part of author's collection.*

Photos

Pushmataha, Mississippi, Choctaw War Chief whose grandson served in the Confederate Army. Choctaw ledgend says: "The winds blew, the rain fell, the thunder roarded, the lighting struck a huge white oak tree and out stepped Pushmataha his rifle on his sholder." (Photo from Collection of the Museum Division Mississippi Department of Archives and History, Jackson, Mississippi).

Cherokee Chief and Confederate General Stand Watie He commanded the last Confederate ground forces to surrender. (Photo courtesy of Oklahoma Historical Society).

When Rebel Was Cool. From the late 1950s to mid-60s the South was celebrating the centennial of the so-called Civil War. Hundreds of southern schools participated in this historic event, many by proudly displaying the Confederate flag. Artist Jerry McWilliams, original part of author's collection.

The Dixie Division Honor Guard circa 1950. Our older brother, Alton Kennedy, was a member of the U. S. Army National Guard Dixie Division. (Photo Wikipedia Commons).

The Dixie Division Band. (Photo Wikipedia Commons).

Sinking of the USS Cairo. Artwork by Jerry McWilliams. My Great Grandfather, John Wesley Kennedy, 38th Mississippi Inf. CSA, was in a rifle-pit on the Yazoo River when they sunk this Yankee gunboat.

Mom holding Alton and Dad. Photo taken 1938. Corner of old Kennedy house seen in upper left.

The GM&O Rebel Route had several "Rebels" beginning in 1935. Photo courtesy of www.rebelrails.com; http://www.rebelrails.com/store/index. php?l=product_list&c=42

Photos

Grandfather Theodore Prentiss Kennedy holding shotgun circa 1909 – His Grandson, Donald Kennedy, is holding the same shotgun, 2019. Theodore's father was private John Wesley Kennedy, of the 38th Mississippi Inf., C.S.A.

Ron defending Mississippi's state flag on MS Public Broadcasting 2017.

Rev. Robert Bradford, Member of Parliament, Northern Ireland and his wife Nora. A personal friend who urged me to always be proud of the South's Scotch-Irish heritage. Rev. Bradford was assassinated by the IRA in 1981. (Photo Keystone Press/Alamy Stock Photo).

Chapter 22:

MAKING DO IN HARD TIMES

HARD TIMES WERE the norm for those of us who grew up in the rural South, at least to the mid-1960s. I recall how men patched inner tubes with multiple hot patches until there was little room left on the inner tube for the next patch. That was before tubeless tires were invented. *Back in the day*, the key to survival was to "make do as best you can with what you have." Many a family lived by the motto "fix it, repair it, or do without." When a farmer's truck tire wore thin and a hole appeared on part of the tire, he would put a *boot* inside the tire to cover the hole, replace the inner tube, and continue using the tire. It was not just truck and car tires that got patches. It was very common at school to see boys wearing old blue jeans with knee patches; shoes with worn-out soles were not thrown away; they were brought to the shoe repair shop and resoled, and no one took offense when someone gave them hand-me-down clothing.

I recall getting hand-me-down shirts and jeans from cousins whose folks moved to Oregon. Some of the Oregon hand-me-downs were too big for us. Mom took them to a black family that lived close by who had young boys. She also took some of our shirts that no longer fit us and gave the hand-me-down clothes to the black family. Mom and the black lady grew up together. When Mom was a young girl, the black lady's family sharecropped a farm close to where granddaddy was sharecropping. It was not unusual to ride by their house and see young black boys wearing our hand-me-down shirts while at the same time, we were wearing our cousin's hand-me-down shirts. It has often been said that "Hard times create strong people, strong people create good times, good times create weak people, weak people create hard times." One thing is for sure: the people of the South have lived through more than our share of "hard times."

When Rebel Was Cool

When you are cash poor, you learn to take care of your tools. Farmers kept their plows under a shed. They knew how to repair them if they were damaged. To lose a tool was as bad as throwing money away. Dad told us about one time when his father was working on the shed that covered their water well. He was using a hatchet to trim a piece of sap-wood. He sat the tool down and then accidentally knocked it off the ledge and into the well—the well should have been covered. The well was a thirty-foot-deep hand-dug well. The water level at the bottom was around four to five feet. When the hatchet went down the well, it did not make a splash. There was a cypress frame at the bottom that kept the dirt from caving off into the water collection area. Dad volunteered to go down and feel around the cypress ledge to see if he could find the hatchet. With that, they tied a rope to Dad's legs and lowered him down, head first to the level of the cypress planking at the bottom. He located and retrieved the hatchet. Who, today, would do such a foolish thing just to reclaim a simple hatchet? But back then, it was not foolish—it was necessity born of hard times.

Even in hard times, our people knew how to enjoy themselves. Granddaddy Kennedy loved to hunt and fish. After the crops were *laid-by*, he loaded up the entire family on to a wagon pulled by a team of mules, and they spent a week down on the Pearl River fishing. During the winter, he spent time in the woods hunting squirrels and rabbits. Notice how even his fun times included activities that produced food for the family. Dad told us about how they dug up sassafras roots. Grandmother Kennedy cleaned the roots, boiled them down, added a sweetener such as molasses, and made a form of sassafras tea—tasting and smelling similar to root beer.

Uncle Lloyd and Dad managed to acquire a second-hand, rusty, Model T. Uncle Lloyd finished high school but was still single. Uncle Lloyd thought of himself as a race car driver. He wanted to see how fast the Model T would go as they approached the little village of Rockport. No doubt he wanted to impress other young folks who might be there. The suspension system on a Model T is not much more than buggy springs. As Uncle Lloyd bounced the Model T over the railroad tracks in Rockport and attempted to make a sharp curve to the left, the bouncing Model T flipped over. Dad was thrown out as it rolled over but was unharmed except for hitting his head on a tree root. A crowd of local youngsters helped them roll the car back over on all four tires, and off they went—not even a dent in the thing! That was back when they used real metal in car bodies—but no seatbelts!

Shortly after the Rockport "roll-over," they decided to make a trip to the Mississippi State Fair in Jackson. They wanted to go because they knew there would be a lot of girls there. But they knew that their chances of catching the eye of any of the girls were small in the old rusty

Making Do in Hard Times

Spur RR track circa 1930s Mississippi. (Photo courtesy of MS Rails http://www.msrailroads.com).

Model T. They solved the problem by using black shoe polish to paint the T Model black—which was the only color available for any of Henry Ford's early T Models. It worked well until they were on the way home and got caught in a thunderstorm. They got a lot of good-natured ribbing, but it was fun, and they both enjoyed retelling the tale—which always seemed to change a little with each telling.

Donald and I spent a lot of time in the woods hunting and fishing on Peggy Creek. Early on, we noticed what looked like railroad trestle pilings in the middle of the creek over on Uncle Lloyd's land. We asked Dad about it. He said that when he was a young teenager, a logging company built a spur railroad track through the community. Those pilings were all that was left of the old spur railroad that crossed Peggy Creek. He told us that the logging company was mainly interested in cutting pine trees, especially the old-growth virgin longleaf pines. He said the logging company did not pay them much for the logs, but when you are an impoverished Southerner, you will take whatever you can get. It was better than nothing. After extensive logging, all that was left of Mississippi's once virgin forest was heart pine stumps. I remember how Donald and I sat on the back porch at dusk with very little light remaining, and as we looked at those tall heart pine stumps, they seemed to move! The ones in Uncle Frank's pasture had a very creepy habit of moving around all night long and then getting back in place by sun up!

The South's virgin forest cut down and shipped up North. (Photo courtesy of MS Rails http://www.msrailroads.com).

Years later, even those old heart pine stumps—the last reminder of the South's vast pre-War expanse of virgin forest—were sold to companies that processed them into turpentine. When researching for our first book, "The South Was Right," we found documentation of how the people of Mississippi, as well as the rest of the South, cut down their entire inheritance of virgin forest in an attempt to pull themselves out of post-War poverty. The logs were sawed into lumber and shipped up North during the North's post-War economic expansion, referred to as the Gilded Age. The South's virgin forests are gone—but the poverty remains. *Vae Victus*—woe to the conquered. *Vae Victus* is what the Roman Empire told those it invaded and conquered. It is true for all people regardless of which empire does the invading and conquering.

Granddaddy Berry lost his farm due to the Great Depression that began in 1929. He, like most other Southern farmers, had borrowed money from the bank to *make a crop*, but when Wall Street crashed, the price of cotton went to the lowest ever in his lifetime. Because he, like many other Southern farmers, was unable to repay the bank, he had to give up the title to his land. He and his family became homeless sharecroppers. They were more fortunate than most. His brother-in-law had a farm and a good house that he was not using. After a spell as a homeless sharecropper, Granddaddy Berry was able to begin sharecropping his brother-in-law's unused farm and live in the vacant house. Unlike other sharecroppers, Granddaddy and Grandmother Berry and family were living in a house owned by a direct relative (Granddaddy's brother-in-law); therefore, they did not have to move to a new farm each year or two as did most sharecroppers. Great Uncle George Little's generosity is an example of how *kith and kin* take care of each other.

Mom told us that during spring and summer, her wake-up alarm was hearing her father outside before sunrise sharpening the hoes that she and her brothers and sisters would be using all day in the cotton field. After sharpening the hoes, he harnessed the mule he used to plow the cotton field, ate breakfast with the family; and then, all would head to the cotton field. Even to her dying day, Mom said that she hated to hear the sound of a hoe being sharpened! She said that every year in early spring, her mother inspected all the girls' straw hats. If they were not in good shape, she had Granddaddy buy a new one. She wanted to make sure her girls did not get too much sun on their faces while working in the cotton fields. *Making a living* for sharecroppers required the full effort of the entire family. It was "hard times," but working together and with firm faith in God's eternal love, they made a good life for themselves.

Making Do in Hard Times

Our Berry grandparents lived in the borrowed house for the rest of their lives. Every Sunday after church, we traveled the short distance to "their" house to visit. I recall one Christmas overhearing Granddaddy Berry lamenting to Mom "I wish I could give my grandchildren a Christmas present but I don't have two nickels in my pocket that I could rub together." Even though they were forced into poverty by economic conditions beyond their control or understanding, they none-the-less raised five children, all of whom became successful and valued members of their communities.

The rural South was the last region of the United States to gain novelties such as electric lights and telephones. Although our local church had electric lights and ceiling fans, I remember, as a young child, seeing small shelves on the walls inside the church. I asked Mom what they were, and she casually replied that they were the shelves that once held the *coal oil* lamps used for light before the church had electric lights. Our house had electric lights from the day Dad built it—around 1946. I recall our neighbor, Mr. Martin Page, did not get electrical power to his house until Donald and I were in grade school—around 1955. Telephones were not available in our community until the early 1960s. Mom and Dad could not afford a phone until after Donald and I had graduated from high school (1965). The gravel road in front of our house was not paved until sometime after 1960. Progress was slow in the rural South not because we did not want progress but because we could not afford it. Poverty is a hard taskmaster—although we never considered ourselves poor. Relative to the rest of the United States, we were poor as measured by material wealth, but we were rich in ways the world could not then and still cannot understand.

Times were hard, but you did not give up; you endured, persevered, and trusted that the Good Lord would see you through. Many a Saturday morning, we helped Dad shell corn and take it to the grist mill to have it processed into cornmeal. We paid for the processing by

Goose neck hoe & Grub hoe

shares—the grist mill owner got one pound, and we got three pounds or a ratio of 1:3. Corn was a very important staple in the diet of rural Southerners. You always took special care to harvest the corn when it was dry and immediately put it in the corn crib where it stayed dry. Rats and mice would get into the corn crib and eat some of the corn. Many folks solved the rat problem by catching a Kingsnake and putting it in the corn crib. In no time at all, the snake solved the rat problem. Kingsnakes are non-poisonous snakes that eat *varmits* (varmints) such as rats. They will also attack, kill and eat poisonous snakes. Dad never allowed us to harm a kingsnake. But Mom hated snakes, so we depended on a set of hungry barn cats to do the job in our corn crib. The important thing was to take care of your food supply—even if you have no money, if you take care of your food stock, you will not go hungry.

The only "investments" our folks ever made was investing in livestock. Chickens were purchased as *bitties* (newly hatched chicks), kept in the chicken brooder, until they grew into juvenile chickens called pullets, and then turned loose to free-range. We fed them a small amount of corn every afternoon, mainly to be able to check on them and make it easy to catch them when needed. Some were kept to replace old hens that no longer produced eggs; others were eaten by the family and some sold. Our cattle "herd" was Dad's primary farm investment, but it never exceeded eight or nine cows and calves. Once a year, a young calf (steer) was taken to the slaughter house—we never slaughtered beef cattle ourselves. Others were taken to market. Dad saved part of the sale price and purchased young calves to bring back to the farm and start the cycle again. We also had hogs. They were kept to be slaughtered on the farm for our own use. We slaughtered our hogs ourselves until we purchased a freezer. By that time, we were "prosperous" enough that we could afford to have our hogs processed at the slaughter house, bring the wrapped meat home, and freeze it.

Corn sheller similar to one used by Kennedy Twins. (Photo taken at MS AG Museum Jackson, MS).

Making Do in Hard Times

In hard times, the family is always threatened by a sudden down turn in the economy or a loss of an investment animal(s). Even healthy-looking animals can become sick or get injured and die. It is hard for folks today to realize the psychological impact the loss of even one farm animal can have on a family that depends on a few animals to augment the family's disposal income. Such a loss is not like the loss of a family pet. It would be more like the loss of a large portion of your bank account or retirement fund. It happened to our family, and it took a lot of work to replace the loss. I will never forget the look of distress and anguish on Mom's and Dad's faces when we had to drag a dead cow off into the woods. The cow fell into a ditch and died. We spent several days looking for the missing cow, only to find her when it was too late to save her. It also brought to life the Bible saying that it is OK to work on Sunday if your ox has fallen in a ditch, and you are working to save your ox. But despite the financial loss, we persevered.

Mom and Dad had a lot of experience with the tragedies of life in the rural South. Mom watched as her father was reduced from a proud landowning small farmer to a broken in spirit, homeless sharecropper. Dad's twin sister died shortly after she was born, his brother Virgil die after falling out of the family's buggy, and he watched his mother die from TB. When the Great Depression was at its height, he and Mom moved into a one room apartment in Jackson, Mississippi. Dad managed to get a job working for a few dollars a day at Mississippi Steel. They used the major part of his salary to pay off the mortgage on the farm, thereby saving Dad's limited inheritance. Although it was hard work for little pay, Dad always counted it as gain because he learned to weld while working there. He then managed to get a job in the ship yards in New Orleans, where he made enough money to pay for the construction of the house in which Donald and I were born. Note: Mom and Dad saved enough money to build their house without going into debt—the Great Depression had taught them a cruel lesson about too much debt.

World War II broke out while Mom and Dad were living in New Orleans. Dad had a job working for a shipyard. He was 32 years old—too old to join the army but he worked to build the Higgins boats that were used in the D-Day landing in Europe and the Pacific. By 1945, manpower for the military became so limited that Dad got a notice that the military would be drafting men his age, but World War II ended before they began drafting the older men—Dad was 36. Dad was too young to serve in World War I and too old to serve in World War II but many of his family and Mom's family did serve during these wars. Many of the Kennedy Twins' children, nephews and nieces have also served in the U. S. military.

Our grandparents Kennedy and Berry, Mom and Dad, and even Donald and I all lived through hard times, but we never thought of ourselves as being "victims." With the help of the Good Lord, we simply picked up our load and carried it as best we could, never being resentful against God or man. (Well, maybe I became a little resentful toward Yankees, but that was well after I grew-up and learned just how unfairly they were treating us). The experience of our *kith and kin*, both past and present, taught Donald and me that life is a struggle, that *nothing good ever comes cheaply*. We knew through sound preaching of the Gospel that even the spiritual salvation we freely received was not really free because it cost God the life of His Only Begotten Son. Religion and spiritual faith are essential for a people to be able to turn hard times into bearable times while always maintaining the hope of one day having "good times."

I recall Aunt Vivian in the last days of her life when she was housebound and unable to attend church, yet every Sunday, she sat on her back porch and listened to the singing coming from the church across the *holler*. She saw hard times but she always kept her faith. She once told me, "There are worse things than dying." In my youth, I could not understand why she said such a thing, but as old age approaches, I now fully understand. Even though we have lived in hard times, life on balance has been good, but God promises something even better for those who truly trust in His Son.

It has often been said that hard times create strong people, strong people create good times, good times create weak people and weak people create hard times. In 2002, John McDermott wrote and sung his version of the Scottish National Anthem, "Scotland the Brave." One line in it struck me when I heard it—it seemed to me to be a fitting warning for the South and the U.S.A. today: "Freedom expires amid softness and sighs." I pray that my Southern *kith and kin* who are descended from those who lived through hard times will not let freedom expire.

Our people, our Southern *kith and kin*, have born up under the emotional stress of hard times. As bad as the physical stress of *making a living* in the impoverished South, as bad as the living conditions were for so many, it all pales when compared to the emotional stress caused by hard times. The eyes of sharecroppers tell the story.

Southern sharecroppers during the Great Depression and the Dust Bowl. Their eyes tell more than words could ever tell. These photos were taken 70 years after a Yankee journalist vowed that the North would punish the South, and we would "see privation in the anxious eyes of mothers and the rags of their children." (Photos courtesy LOC).

Hard Times Come Again No More
(A song written by Stephen Foster).

Let us pause in life's pleasures and count its many tears,
While we all sup sorrow with the poor;
There's a song that will linger forever in our ears;
Oh hard times come again no more.

[chorus] Tis the song, the sigh of the weary,
Hard Times, hard times, come again no more
Many days you have lingered around my cabin door;
Oh hard times come again no more.

While we seek mirth and beauty and music light and gay,
There are frail forms fainting at the door;
Though their voices are silent, their pleading looks will say
Oh hard times come again no more.

When Rebel Was Cool

[chorus]

There's a pale drooping maiden who toils her life away,
With a worn heart whose better days are o'er:
Though her voice would be merry, 'tis sighing all the day,
Oh hard times come again no more.

[chorus]

Tis a sigh that is wafted across the troubled wave,
Tis a wail that is heard upon the shore
Tis a dirge that is murmured around the lowly grave
Oh hard times come again no more.

    Soft times — times of material prosperity — produce soft people. The chains of slavery can be gently applied to those who have abandoned their unending duty to be ever vigilant against even the slightest encroachment upon their freedom and liberty. Eventually an apathetic and docile people will learn to love their chains. The idea of freedom frightens those who have allowed themselves to grow accustomed to slavery.

Chapter 23:

RACE RELATIONS IN THE RURAL SOUTH

IN THE RURAL SOUTH, when Donald and I were growing up, folks used to say that there were two types of people in the South; poor whites and poor blacks. Some black Southerners were *better off* than some white Southerners while, some whites were *better off* than some blacks. Even though we were different in skin color, we were all connected by relative poverty—relative to the average American in other parts of the United States. We were also

"*My name is Nelson W. Winbush. My Grandfather fought for the Confederacy and I honor his service.*" The Kennedy Twins were honored to meet Mr. Winbush at a National Sons of Confederate Veterans Reunion. (Photo from Facebook).

connected through our Christian faith. Even though we attended different churches, we none-the-less all professed faith in the same Jesus. Even during the height of *Jim Crow* (racial segregation), white children were taught in Sunday School to sing the song proclaiming, "Jesus loves the little children. Red and yellow, black and white, all are precious in His sight." Our mutual existence in an impoverished condition, a condition of poverty unjustly imposed upon us, and our mutual faith in Jesus Christ united us in ways we did not recognize or understand. What is so mystifying to the Yankee mind is that we (Southerners) could not explain this deeply rooted mutual connection between white and black Southerners. But as is so typical in the Southern psyche—we did not try to explain, examine, or explore it, we simply accepted it.

During the fifteen years in which we grew up—1950 to 1965 (we were born in 1947 but our memories began in 1950)—two significant social events occurred that had a dramatic impact on white and black Southerners. Unfortunately, neither side understood the uniqueness of these events as it related to the other group or how it impacted the thinking (mindset or frame of reference) of each group. During these fifteen years, the white South celebrated the centennial of the War for Southern Independence—incorrectly referred to as the *Civil War*. It was a time of great celebrations and remembering the gallantry and sufferings of our relatives—grandfathers, or great grandfathers. Many a family told and retold stories about their blood relatives who wore the gray in the War for Southern Independence. We all felt like we were there during *the War* because our grand or great-grandparents were there. Their blood flows through our veins—present tense not past tense. Local newspapers published stories and old photographs of the gathering of local Confederate veterans—this was before Yankee corporations bought up most of our local Southern newspapers and turned them into left-wing, anti-South, *scalawag* rags. It was also the time before neo-Marxist professors took over taxpayer funded Southern Universities and began brainwashing our children with postmodernist, neo-Marxist propaganda disguised as education. In many of the old photographs of aged Confederate veterans, published in locally owned newspapers, you would see black, Indian (Native American), or Hispanic veterans. It was a time when we the people of the South were celebrating our family histories. It was a season to remember the honorable heritage of our Southern *kith and kin*. One scholar tried to explain the enthusiasm for this celebration by noting that it is only natural for a people to cling to the past, when they have been robbed of their future.

It was during these same fifteen years—while the white South was celebrating the centennial of *the War*—that the Civil Rights movement took center stage in Southern society. Because the Federal government was pushing the Civil Rights movement (for political purposes), it became almost natural for the children of the fallen Confederacy to resist the Federal government—the same Federal government that made war against our grandfathers and great grandfathers. A substantial, if not a majority, of the white South's sentiment against the Civil Rights movement came from a natural desire to resist the abuses of an all-powerful Federal government. Remember, *Scot-Irish* Southerners live by the feud—insults to the family have a long memory. No doubt, this was not the way black Southerners saw it. And, without a doubt, there were some white Southerners who were motivated by racial hatred—a hatred that was not and is not a natural part of our Southern society. (See definition herein of *cultural distortion*).

Today, the vast majority of the white South supports equal rights for all our citizens. The sincere conversion (bordering on contrition) of the white South from opposition to equal rights under the law to supporting equal rights under the law (regardless of skin color) is the most dramatic success story of the entire Civil Rights movement. It was one of history's greatest, if not the greatest, change of a people's social psychology—a radical change in the foundational principle (white rule) upon which they based their society. An entire population changed its fundamental rationale for the functioning of its society as it relates to matters of race. What makes it more dramatic is that this change was accomplished in a very short time.

One of the main reasons for this conversion is that white Southerners remembered the song they sang in Sunday School "Jesus loves the little children...red, yellow, black, and white, all are precious in His sight." They sat under the preaching of the Gospel which requires all Christians to "Do unto others as you would have them do unto you," (Matthew 7:12) and Jesus' own admonition "By this shall all men know that ye are my disciples, if ye have love one to another," (John 13:35).

Two instances of domestic terrorism in the South, one in 1963 the other in 2015, provides heartbreaking (as it relates to the death of innocent brothers and sisters in Christ) but clear evidence of the change in the psyche of white Southerners. This evidence can be obtained by contrasting the difference between how white Southern society responded to the 1963 Birmingham, Alabama, church bombing that killed four black children, and the 2015 killing of nine black church members in Charleston, South Carolina. In 1963, there was white outrage to the killing of "little black children attending Sunday School," but the outrage was expressed privately, low voice level, and behind closed doors. The reason for the 1963 silent outrage was that to express outrage against such attacks back then would have exposed white individuals or churches to a similar attack. Fear within the white community was the main reason for silent outrage back then. This fear is not that different from the fear today that prevents many blacks from working with the police to solve crimes in their neighborhood—crimes committed by organized and violent gangs that will use violence against anyone who provides information to the police.

Now go forward 52 years to 2015. When the Charleston, SC attack occurred, there was immediate, forceful, public, outrage expressed from white Southern churches, ministers, social leaders, political leaders, and private individuals. Why the difference between 1963 and 2015? The white South was taught the meaning of "Do unto others as you would have them do unto you." Today, the overwhelming majority of the South's population understands that all Southerners are *kith and kin*—an attack on one of our brothers or sisters in Christ is an attack on all of us—skin color plays no part in the expression of our outrage and demand for justice. And as Southerners, we live by the feud—the attacker who single-handedly murdered nine people at Emanuel Church in Charleston, South Carolina, must pay with his life. *In short order*, he was captured, tried, convicted, and sentenced to death. (The admonition that we are all *kit and kin* is also true for Southerners of the Jewish faith. An attack upon Southerners of the Jewish faith or their synagogues would meet with similar outrage and an insistence upon appropriate punishment for the offending party).

A few evil people have misused the flags and other symbols of the Confederate States of America. Those of us who honor our Southern heritage have no way to prevent evil people from misusing our Southern flags and symbols. But just because evil people misappropriate the Confederate flag is no reason to ban the display of our flag. Evil people have misappropriated the Holy Bible, the Christian Cross, and the United States flag, but that is no justification to ban their display or label the people who honor those symbols as being intrinsically evil—also known as guilt by association. We should judge people by their actions, the content of their character, not by the color of the flag they happen to be waving. Unfortunately, and for political reasons, secular humanists, and left-of-center political activists do not care to make this fundamental and logical distinction. They find it politically convenient to label all who treasure their Southern heritage as racists. But this is far from the reality that Donald and I lived growing up in the rural South. Outside of political issues: What was the relationship between black and white Southerners?

I recall one day when Donald and I went to the small general store in Oma, Mississippi. It must have been some time in 1955. Several white men were sitting on the *loafers' bench* outside the store. An elderly black lady was approaching the door at the same time we were. She halted and stood back while Dad reached out and opened the door, but instead of us going in, Dad waited for the black lady to go in while he held the door open for her. I still remember her words as she said, "Why, thank you, sir." (The "sir" sounded more like "sur" which was common for both black and white at the time). Before we could go through the door, one of the white characters on the *loafers' bench* asked Dad in a very harsh tone, "You holding the door open for that (N-word)?" Dad stopped, looked at the man, and replied, "The Bible says we never know when we might be helping one of God's angels. That black woman may well be one of God's angels." With that short sermon—given mainly for the benefit of his sons—the three of us went into the store. Mom and Dad were insistent that we understood that regardless of skin color—our souls have no color. But don't get the idea that Mom and Dad were trendy social justice warriors—they were traditional, Bible believing, conservative Southerners. As with most Southerners, they believed that change would come to our society, but it would come in a slow and manageable way. Anything that hinted at political radicalism was anathema (abhorrent) to their way of thinking.

While working in Vicksburg, Mississippi, in 1968, I was told the story of how an elderly black man saved a number of people when the bridge that crossed the Big Black River collapsed one night during a storm that occurred in the 1950s. I have no way to verify the story, but it had been told and retold many times by the time I first heard it. Even if the story is not true, it was certainly a widely circulated folktale that demonstrates the respect black and white folks have or should have for one and another. It challenges those Southerners who hear the folktale to emulate the hero by being a useful part of society even if it costs you the slings and arrows of the ignorant and hateful. It encourages us to always be willing to "help our fellow man." It also vividly demonstrates the harmful impact that racial hatred can have on the individual who is possessed by such hatred. It was a common type of parable that was told for the benefit of white and black folks alike—a way to unconsciously encourage the social attitude of *kith and kin* among our people.

According to this folktale, an elderly black man was awakened one stormy night by the sound of the bridge over the Big Black River crashing into the raging river. He immediately lit his *coal oil* lantern, got dressed, and walked down the road to check the bridge. Upon seeing it completely collapsed, he posted himself in the middle of the road at the top of the hill to stop oncoming cars. The storm was crashing about him with lightning, thunder, wind, and rain, but he stayed at his self-assigned post waving down vehicles as they sped toward the collapsed bridge. God only knows how many lives he saved that dark and stormy night. But as one car approached, the driver slowed down, swung the car over to the road's shoulder, drove around the man and cursed at him, demanding "get out of my way you damn (N-word)" and sped onward to his watery death at the bottom of the hill. This black man remained at his post even after being insulted. He

The Kennedy Twins with Southern Patriot Teresa Roan 2018.

did it because it was the right — as in Christian — thing to do. The moral of the story was clear to all who heard it. We do our Christian duty, even though the world may insult and hate us, and hatred, though cruel and unfair for the target of the hatred, will eventually bring far greater destruction upon the person or society possessed by hatred. I have heard similar types of stories told all across the South.

As a young child, I was made aware of another story. This story I know is true. It involved a poor white sharecropping family. I knew the members of that poor sharecropping family because the family was my Grandfather and Grandmother Berry's family. My mother, her brothers, and her sisters were participants in the event.

On the farm next to the one that Granddaddy Berry was sharecropping was a family of black sharecroppers. The father became an alcoholic, abandoned the family, and eventually died. The mother became ill and died leaving one pre-teen boy an orphan with no one to take care of him. Granddaddy and Grandmother brought the young boy to their house, made a place for him, and for all practical purposes, they "adopted" the young black boy. All the family called him "Boy," which, to them, was a term of endearment. Remember, the tone of voice and facial expression can determine the meaning or intent of a word. As he grew older, he asked them to call him Boyce. I knew him as Boyce — my black uncle. This all occurred in the 1930s in rural Mississippi at a time when *Jim Crow* segregation was both law and custom. Yet, here was a family of poor white sharecroppers who took on the responsibility of feeding and caring for another child during the South's endless "hard times." The motivation for doing so was that it was the right — as in Christian — thing to do.

After he reached manhood, Boyce moved close to Jackson, Mississippi, and eventually became the owner of a general store. Just like the rest of Granddaddy Berry's children, he became relatively successful. At least once every year on a Sunday afternoon, Boyce brought his family by to check on Granddaddy and Grandmother Berry. During the year, different uncles or aunts would hear news from Boyce and share it with the family during our Sunday visits. Years later, when Granddaddy Berry died, I recall my uncles and aunts asking each other if anyone had called Boyce to tell him the sad news. I recall being at the funeral home when Boyce came in to grieve with the rest of the family. Up to that point, everyone held up well, controlling our grief while quietly visiting and doing our best to comfort Grandmother. I recall someone saying, "Oh! Y'all look. There's Boyce." Boyce came over to the open casket, looked down at Granddaddy Berry's body, and began to sob while slowly saying, "He's the only daddy I ever knew." All decorum was swept away as everyone joined Boyce's sobbing and crying. What a demonstration

Race Relations in the Rural South

of the unique and inscrutable relations between the races in the segregated South. None of us could explain it; none of us saw a need to explain it; we merely accepted it.

Perhaps that is why Donald and I did not find it unusual when we found out, while researching for our book "Was Jefferson Davis Right," that during the War, President Jefferson Davis and his wife *took in* (befriended) an abandoned black boy (Jim Limber) and made him a part of the Davis family. They filed papers documenting him as a free person of color. He remained a part of the Confederacy's First Family until the end of the War. Jim Limber was with President Davis and the rest of the Davis family when the Yankees captured President Davis. The Yankee troops kidnapped Jim even though the Davis children and Mrs. Davis put up a vocal and the children a physical effort to keep Jim with the rest of the family. After falling into Yankee hands, Jim Limber disappeared and was never heard of again. Yankee "historians" and "scholars" will never tell you such stories — that is why it is so important that we do our part to make sure these truths of history are passed down to our people generation by generation.

Jim Limber, circa 1865. (From photo held by Confederate Museum, Richmond Virginia. Artwork by Charles Hayes).

Years later, when I was watching "Gone With the Wind," the memory of the scene with Boyce at the funeral home was the key to my understanding of an otherwise odd scene in that movie. In the movie there is a scene that occurs shortly after the end of *the War* when Scarlet's family, once wealthy, was reduced to poverty. Scarlet's father, Gerald O'Hara, dies, and of course, the entire family is grieving with the outpouring of many tears. Then enters one of the former slaves who remained with the family after *the War*. When he finds out about the death of his former master, he breaks down in tears. Scarlet, hardened by war, death, destruction, and poverty, immediately orders the servant to leave the room declaring, "I can stand anybody's tears — except yours." Critics of the South would see this scene as representing racial hatred because Scarlet "callously and insultingly ordered a black man out of the room because he, a black man, dared to shed tears in her presence." But as my Grandmother Berry once told me about Yankees, "they ant us." They don't understand us because they "ant us." What Scarlet did is the exact opposite of hatred. It represented a human connection between black and white Southerners that is impossible to explain—it is merely accepted.

Shortly after *the War*, the Yankee Congress sent a former Union General, who was also a socialist from Germany, down South on a mission to report back to Congress on the conditions in the conquered South. His report no doubt shocked and confused the Yankee Congressmen. He wrote that generations of slavery had not taught black Southerners to hate white Southerners. He noted that when former slaves met former masters on the street, there was a genuine expression of concern expressed each for the other and sincere inquiries about how each was doing. What centuries of slavery could not do—teach blacks to hate whites—a few short years of Yankee Reconstruction and subsequent political domination of the South did in some ways accomplish. Post-War Republican politics established the system of *divide and rule* as a means by which the North could control the South. *Divide and rule* is a technique for controlling the people of an invaded and conquered nation. All empires do it—the Yankee empire is no different. Donald and I discuss this sad aspect of the South's political history in "Punished With Poverty-the Suffering South," and "Yankee Empire: Aggressive Abroad and Despotic at Home."

Years after our Berry grandparents passed away, I had another personal experience that demonstrated the respect and love that existed between the races in the rural South. Mom's oldest sister, Aunt Lilly Cole Holyfield (1913-2010) and her husband, Uncle Robert Holyfield (1911-1988), *took-in* (befriended) a black man who was destitute. Uncle Robert owned several large commercial chicken houses. One day as he was leaving the local general store, he noticed a black man sitting on the *loafers' bench*. He had seen the man several times on previous days but did not recognize him. The store owner said that the black man's name was Carswell—Uncle Robert's surviving family member cannot recall Carswell's last name. He appeared a few weeks back and spent his days sitting out in front of the store. On Uncle Robert's next trip to the store, Carswell was again sitting there on the *loafer's bench*. Uncle Robert asked him if he would like to earn a little spending money helping him at his chicken farm. He appeared to be around Uncle Robert's age and in good health. The black man's face lit up with excitement, and he gladly agreed. Uncle Robert found out that the man was living in a stall of an old barn nearby. He had no "people" (family) to take care of him. He said that now and then, some young relatives would come by and take what little money he had. When the day's work was over, Uncle Robert paid him and told him he could go to which Carswell replied, "But I wants to stay here."

Uncle Robert and Aunt Lily Cole went to work, making a place for the man. They made sure his social security check went to his new "home," established a banking account for him, and made sure he signed up for Medicare. From that day until years later when his "family" came and took him away, he had a comfortable, secure place to call home and plenty of Aunt Lily Cole's home-cooked food to eat.

Carswell (last name unknown)

What was the motivation for such kindness? Very simple: it was the right — as in Christian — thing to do. The South was, and still is, full of such untold stories of human kindness — white to black as well as black to white. Unfortunately, because we lost *the War*, it is impossible to tell our side of the story. News stories about church burnings or lynching's will make headlines or lead stories in the mainline media and be repeated for years without end. But such evil things, while they happened, they were the exception, not the rule. Yet, the world does not know the truth. The world does not know because the South's enemies have purposefully hidden (censored) the truth from the world. Because of Yankee censorship the world misjudges the South as being intrinsically evil.

In 1962, Donald and I were in high school in Wesson. At that time the high school was on the campus of Copiah Lincoln Junior College (now referred to as Copiah Lincoln Community College). The Civil Rights movement was at its height. A new student had recently arrived from somewhere up North — I think it was Chicago. I'm not sure what his connection to our part of the world was, perhaps he had relatives living in Wesson. It did not take long for the young man to stand out as a typical Yankee; he spoke with a typical Yankee accent and always seemed to be in a rush. He often mocked our accents or the use of colloquialisms. He laughed out loud when one student asked him, "Will you hope me out?" "Hope" in ancient usage of the *Scotch-Irish* people also means "help." It was very seldom used, even in my day as a youth, but I still understood it when used in that manner. It was strange to us that the young Northerner was extremely eager to go to town (Wesson) on Saturday afternoon. Wesson was a sleepy little rural Southern village with one stop-light. We all wondered what he wanted to see in Wesson. On Monday, when Donald and I arrived for school (high school, not college), a number of the students at school—college and high school—were laughing about the Yankee's disappointing trip to Wesson the prior Saturday afternoon.

You see, this Yankee thought he knew all about the evil South. After all, he read about the church burnings, lynch mobs, and other evil racist acts "routinely" committed by the *rank and file* white South against our black neighbors. He could not wait to see how white Southerners did not allow blacks Southerners to walk on the sidewalks in our cities and towns. He fully expected to see white men pushing black men and women off the sidewalks and out into the middle of the streets. One simple trip to town caused all of his Yankee-inspired illusions about the evil South to come crashing down. When I heard about this incident, I could not help but recall the numerous times in Hazlehurst when Mom stopped on the sidewalk and talked with black ladies she knew growing up. They exchanged news about mutual acquaintances and news about family affairs. The poor Yankee lad had no frame of reference or means to make an accurate evaluation of our Southern society. It was not his fault, though. Because the South is a conquered nation, we have no way to tell our side of the story. The only information the young Yankee had about us was what he gained from reading anti-Southern, Yankee newspapers, and journals, and watching Yankee-controlled TV. This scenario is not new—it happened in centuries past.

One of the many slanderous pre-War books about the South was Harriet Beecher Stowe's book "Uncle Tom's Cabin." Harriet Stowe was from New England. She was from a family that was politically and socially active. Her direct knowledge about the South was very limited. She did make a short visit to the upper South but spent most of her time while on the plantation shut up in her room reading. She never visited the lower South. Her primary "knowledge" of the South and the institution of slavery as practiced in the South was from reading hyper-critical Yankee newspaper and journal accounts— not to mention a large volume of radical abolitionist propaganda. She used this type of biased anti-South "information" to construct the fictional account detailed in "Uncle Tom's Cabin." It would be similar to me writing a book about modern day Chicago using only the accounts about Chicago I read in the newspaper. The one thing that is constant—back then and today—is that newspapers and other mass media prefer to headline violent crime and other negative stories because such stories garner more readership—which is in itself a poor commentary on human beings in general. But even though Chicago has an impoverished ghetto area with a terrible murder and crime rate, that is not the totality of modern-day Chicago. I have no love for big Yankee cities, but anyone who knows the truth about Chicago must admit that crime, drugs, and murder are not the totality of Chicago. Chicago has a grand business center, numerous museums, art galleries, Universities, and exclusive suburbs where a large middle and upper-middle-class live. If I were to write a book describing conditions about Chicago using only "facts" that I gained from newspapers, the account would not be accurate and would, in fact, be a slander on the vast majority who live or work there. Yet, this is what Harriet Beecher Stowe did to the South. Her slanderous depiction of extreme cruelty by Southerners against slaves was gist for radical abolitionists as they ginned up Northern hatred for the South. It is also one of the reasons Yankees thought that as soon as they invaded the Confederate States of America, *the War* would end because of massive slave revolts. But massive slave revolts never happened.

In 1992, I was privileged to become friends with Dr. Lennard Haynes, Sr. He was a professor at Southern University in Baton Rouge, Louisiana. Southern University in Baton Rouge was, and still, is a predominantly black University. Dr. Haynes shared his life experience with me, and in many ways, it was not that dissimilar from my experience growing up in *Dixie*. I recall a speech he gave to the National Sons of Confederate Veterans in which he proudly proclaimed that "Johnny Reb was not just white; he was also black." Dr. Haynes was proud of his Southern roots and the kinship he felt for his white Southern *kith and kin*. He told me about when he was studying at College in Boston, Massachusetts. He said he needed a part-time job to support himself, but no one there would hire him. He finally got a job when he was hired by a man in Boston who migrated there from the South. He encouraged us to continue the struggle to tell the truth about our mutual home—*Dixie*.

Mom & Aunt Lilly Cole (Berry) Holyfield trying to avoid Civil Rights demonstrators

During the mid-1960s when the Civil Rights movement was at its height it was common to see black demonstrators in Southern towns and cities. Mom and Aunt Lilly Cole (Berry) Holyfield were in Jackson, Mississippi, doing some shopping one Saturday. Unknown to them it was the same day when a large civil rights demonstration was being held on Capitol street in Jackson. It was a time of great social anxiety and mistrust between black and white Southerners. They decided to take a side street to avoid the demonstrators. As they walked down the street a large black man turned the corner and approached them. They were initially afraid, what should they do? Should they cross the street to avoid the black man? Suddenly the man picked-up his pace coming toward them and with a big grin on his face he hollered out—"what are *yawl* doing here on a day like today?" To their relief it was their "adopted" black brother Boyce! All laughed out loud. They explained that they were trying to avoid the crowd on Capitol Street and Boyce said he was doing the same thing because he had to get back to his store. "Just listen to them over there," Boyce declared, "they just trying to get what we always had."

The leftwing, politically correct, crowd claim that the South's pride in its Civil War history, especially its celebration in the 1950s-1960s of the War's centennial was an act of opposition to the Civil Rights Movement. The truth is that Southerners were celebrating the valor of their parents, grandparents and great grandparents who wore the gray in the War for Southern Independence. This pride was demonstrated on the cover of "Sports Illustrated College Edition" September 24, 1962 that proudly displayed a photograph of Ole Miss majorettes dressed in gray, quasi Confederate, military uniforms, carrying Confederate Battle Flags, and the U. S. Army DD military patch proudly worn by the Dixie Division during World War I, World War II and into the late 1950s. It has often been noted that Dr. Martin Luther King never marched against the memory of Confederate Veterans, Confederate monuments, or the Flags of the Confederate States of America. He did urge us to judge people by the content of their character, not by some arbitrary thing such as skin color. While Dr. King preached tolerance, modern-day leftists preach and enforce intolerance for all things Southern. Artwork on left, by Jerry McWilliams, DD U.S. military patch was worn by our older brother, Alton Kennedy, and artwork to right by Charles Hayes. Photo of "Sports Illustrated College Edition" September 24, 1962 available at: https://www.si.com/vault/issue/43611/0

Chapter 24:

HOWARD DIVINITY
COPIAH COUNTY'S BLACK CONFEDERATE

Uncle Seth fought the Yankees (C. Whittington, artist).

[The following story is taken from the collection of true stories told by Uncle Seth in my book "Uncle Seth Fought the Yankees." Uncle Seth is fictional but his stories are true, based on first hand written accounts].

It was a beautiful, warm April 26, 1917 morning. Uncle Seth had come to Hazlehurst with his grandson, Lloyd, to give the young man a chance to see the annual parade of Hazlehurst school children as they marched to the Confederate cemetery to honor the men who wore the gray in the War for Southern Independence. April 26 had been selected in Mississippi as the day when, once a year, the living would pay homage to the dead soldiers of the Confederate States of America. Mississippians would always claim that their ladies were the first Southern ladies to begin the tradition of Decoration Day, which would later be known as Memorial Day. Uncle Seth and Lloyd followed the children's procession as they marched in order toward the cemetery. Each child carried a collection of Paul Scarlet red roses in their small hands. It was part of the tradition for the children to stop at Mrs. S.C. Caldwell's home. Once there they would cut roses from a climbing rose trellis in her yard to decorate the Confederate and two other graves. As they entered the cemetery, Uncle Seth and Lloyd took off their hats as a sign of respect to the fallen.

"Uncle Seth, look over there," Lloyd spoke in a whisper, "what are those two tombstones doing outside of the chain border marking the resting place of the other soldiers?"

"That's where unknown Yankee soldiers are buried. We did not want to have Yankees lying beside the men they were trying to kill, so we buried them outside the Confederate grave site," responded Uncle Seth. "When the children have placed their red roses on all of our graves, they will also take flowers over to those graves and decorate them because they were soldiers, too."

Each grave was decorated with red roses, and red and white ribbons — the colors of the Confederate Stars and Bars. A Confederate Battle flag was proudly posted at the cemetery's entrance. The children sang *"Dixie"* and a local pastor gave the benediction. This scene would be repeated all across the South, although in the more northern regions of *Dixie*, it would usually occur on June 6, President Jefferson Davis' birthday, because the flowers bloomed much later up there than down in the deep South.

After the benediction as folks were leaving, several of the children came over and asked Uncle Seth if he was "one of our soldiers?" Uncle Seth replied that he was, but he was not nearly as famous as Copiah County's famous Black Confederate, Uncle Howard Divinity. "Now by the way," declared Uncle Seth, *"Yawl* know that Copiah is English for Choctaw words, coi (panther) and apahyah (to call) meaning calling panther. You know Copiah County had both Choctaw and black soldiers fighting for us."

"Come here and I will tell you about Copiah County's black Confederate, a man who made life so much more bearable for those of us who were lucky enough to be in 'his' unit," Uncle Seth said as a way of encouragement to the young children.

"Uncle Howard Divinity — you all know that we refer to elderly black men as Uncle out of respect — well he was one of the last of the 'tree talkers' from deep within Bayou Pierre swamp. He was certainly the last one living here in Copiah County. He claimed to be 108 years old the year he died. A 'tree talker, according to black folklore, is a conjurer with great magical powers. Uncle Howard Divinity claimed he got his powers from his mother who was a witch — perhaps a Voodoo Queen from down in New Orleans. It always seemed strange to us that a man who claimed to be the son of a witch and possessing magical powers would have 'Divinity' as a last name. Well he used his 'powers' to help scavenge many a chicken for his mess mates during *the War*. He was there with us during the entire war. After *the War* he was always in attendance at Annual Reunions and an honored part of our local camp of the United Confederate Veterans. I recall that one

Howard Divinity, Hazlehurst, MS, Confederate Veteran, circa 1920. Divinity on right.(Photo courtesy MS Dept. of Archives and History).

year just before his death; he wanted to attend the Annual Reunion but did not have the financial means necessary. When the ex-service men from Copiah County heard about Uncle Howard Divinity's dilemma, they took up a collection—a love offering as it was called—and paid the cost of Uncle Divinity's trip. Shortly after his last Reunion the old man died. He had no family—other than his Confederate comrades— and no one to pay for his funeral. The Charles E. Hooker chapter of the United Daughters of the Confederacy (UDC) paid for the funeral of Copiah County's Black Confederate. One of the ladies from Copiah County, Ruth Bass, wrote about Uncle Howard in *Scribner's Magazine*. Now that his story has been published in a famous magazine, Uncle Howard Divinity will be remembered long after we have taken our resting place over there," Uncle Seth was pointing over to the Confederate section of the cemetery.

A Word About Mississippi's Choctaw Confederates

Before *the War* Copiah County still had Choctaw Indians living in the county. Major J. W. Pearce in Hazlehurst, Mississippi (now the county seat of Copiah County) organized the First Battalion of Choctaw Indians in 1862. They were sent to Camp Moore in Tangipahoa, Louisiana (just south of McComb, Mississippi) for training.

The famous Choctaw War Chief Pushmataha's grandson Eahantatubbe — he went by his white name of Jack Amos — also served in the Confederate army. Jack and his fellow Choctaw braves were responsible for saving the lives of many Confederate soldiers when a troop train derailed and fell into the raging waters of the Chunkey River. After *the War* the United Confederate Veterans Camp Number 1312 was organized in Meridian, Mississippi. The Camp had sixty-eight white veterans and eighteen Choctaw veterans enrolled. Jack Amos was one of the members. War Chief Pushmataha would have been proud of his grandson. There were also other American Indians who fought for the Confederacy: Cherokee, Chickasaw, Creek, and Seminole.

By the way: The Sons of Confederate Veterans (SCV) was organized in 1896 by the United Confederate Veterans and commissioned to vindicate the cause for which the Confederate Veterans fought. The SCV is one of the oldest active veterans' organizations in the United States — a proud heritage defending a proud heritage.

Chapter 25:

HOW TO SPEAK SOUTHERN REDNECK WORDS AND PHRASES

SOUTHERN AMERICAN ENGLISH (the Southern accent and the unique words and phrases we use in day-to-day conversation) is one of the many distinctive aspects of being a Southerner. Our Southern accent identifies and sets us apart from other Americans. Southern American English includes the unique words and phrases used in everyday conversation and also the manner in which we speak. The voice tone and inflections we give words as we communicate. Many of these unique words and phrases are unfamiliar to those unfortunate folks raised north of the Mason-Dixon line. According to one study, folks speaking Southern American English are part of the U.S.A.'s largest group speaking a regional accent. Southerners use a lot of images, symbols, idioms, and exaggerations in our speech. Embellishing the truth for dramatic effect is perfectly acceptable because the speaker assumes the listener can tell from his voice tone that he is engaging in exaggeration. For example, we may say, "He has enough money to burn a wet mule!" By that, we do not mean that the individual intends to use dollar bills to burn a dead mule but that he has a lot of money—money to "throw away!" Southern comedians are well known for embellishing their stories for the dramatic or comedic effect.

Our Southern speech (accent) is unique within the United States. It is often considered odd and uneducated in the rush, rush world of Yankeedom. Yankee speech is best typified by the hustle and bustle of New York City; the shouting madness on the floor of the Wall Street Stock Exchange; and more recently by an outpouring of crude vulgarities, especially from Hollywood. Yankee speech is, deliberately or unconsciously, tainted with an air of superiority and arrogance for those who do not follow Yankee speech patterns. Yankee speech is more like a jackhammer breaking concrete (loud but effective), whereas

Southern speech is more like the cooing of a dove (soft, gentle, seldom direct, and often confusing to the uninitiated). Southerners tend to speak relatively slowly and softly in an almost musical rhythm—especially to the ears of a Southerner who has been away from home for a long time. There are cultural reasons for the Southern pattern of speech—these reasons are lost to most people today, but the speech pattern or accent remains.

In day-to-day conversation, Southerners often structure their sentences in a conditional manner that tends to soften the message. This "softened message" is often confusing to Yankees who are more direct and to our ears, even abrasive in their speech pattern. For example, a Southern land owner discussing the correctness of the property line with his neighbor would say; "I *recon* (reckon) you could say that the fence line needs to be corrected if you have a mind to question it," or "I wouldn't expect him to keep his word if I were you." This "conditional" way of speaking creates a distance between the speaker's allegation/assertion/claim and the listener's potential reaction. It lowers the feeling or sense of being personally critical of another person. It demonstrates the continuing attitude of respect and courtesy toward the listener verbally, especially when discussing an issue in dispute. Remember, Southerners are descended (by blood or spirit) from the Celtic (*Scotch-Irish*) people who have always been known for carrying weapons and who are quick to take offense and use their weapons if their personal or family honor is questioned or insulted. Speaking slowly, softly, and conditionally among such people is necessary if one desires to live in peace or remain among the living!

Unfortunately, the cultural nuances and uniqueness of our regional language and accent are slowly being removed. Hopefully, the Redneck Dictionary below will help to preserve our unique way of *tawking* (also known as talking) and provide Northerners of good will a useful language guide when visiting or moving down South. By the way, this short dictionary is by no means a complete listing of Southern words and phrases. It merely represents words and phrases I have heard and used all my life.

About as popular as a polecat at a camp meeting: Someone or a thing very unpopular. A polecat is another term for a skunk, and a camp meeting is an outdoor religious gathering.

A-coming: When you see someone or something approaching you. "Them Yankees were brave while they were burning unarmed civilians' homes, but they *show nuff* scattered when they saw General Forrest *a-coming*." Often used in reference to oneself as when Mom calls out and tell you to hurry up. Your reply would be, "I'm *a-coming*." It is also spelled as one word, like it is said "acoming."

A hill of beans: Used as a derogatory term to describe a project or person that will not amount to very much. "That boy won't amount to *a hill of beans.*" Beans are planted in "hills," consisting of three or four seeds in a small hole made every five or six inches on top of a row in the garden. It takes many "hills" of beans to make enough beans to feed a family. One hill of beans will not be enough to feed the chickens, let alone a family.

A mess: A portion of food usually sufficient to feed a family. "Mama, you going to cook us *a mess* of butter beans for *supper*?" In the military, the dining facilities are often referred to as the "Mess Hall." During the War for Southern Independence, soldiers within each Company (a unit consisting of between 60 to 120 men) were divided into small groups called "mess mates." This small group consisted of four to six soldiers. Each group of "mess mates" was responsible for selecting one person to prepare their food. Enough food to feed four to six soldiers was prepared. A mess of greens was enough to feed four to six people.

A passel: A large grouping of items, animals, or people. "There was *a passel* of hogs in grandma's garden."

A spell: A short time. "He just stopped by to visit for *a spell.*" It can also mean a temporary physical or mental condition: "She is OK. She just had a fainting spell."

A stitch in time will save nine: Early correction of a tear on a garment, one or two stitches, will prevent it from becoming worse and thus requiring extensive stitching. Early correction of a personal error will prevent additional harm.

A whistling woman and a crowing hen never come to a good end: In the old days, women of very low morals would whistle at men to attract the attention of possible customers—such immoral women never come to a good end. On the farm, everyone knows that it is natural for roosters to crow. We also know that it is unnatural for a hen to crow, but sometimes they do. When a hen crows, it is taken as a bad sign or an evil omen that death is coming to the farm. To keep the family members safe, the crowing hen was killed (death comes to the farm) and eaten at *supper*. Thus, the crowing hen comes to no good end.

Acre: A common measurement for farmland in the South. During the Middle Ages, it was common to define an acre as the amount of land a peasant could plow with an ox in a day. Later, it was standardized to being equal to 43,560 square feet of land or one furlong (660 feet) by one chain (66 feet). After the unfortunate ending of *the War* during Reconstruction, the newly freed slaves were promised 40 acres and a mule if they voted the Republican ticket. It was one of many false promises made (back then and today) by politicians to impoverished black Southerners—promises they never intended to keep.

Add insult to injury: Taking advantage of an individual who has suffered a loss. "After the bully knocked ole Jim out cold, to add insult to injury, he stole Jim's favorite pocket knife."

Airish: Cold breeze outside or cold room needing heat. "It's airish in here. We need to get the fireplace a going (pronounced as one word 'agoing')."

Alike as two peas in a pod: The Kennedy Twins are well familiar with this expression—we have heard it all our lives. It means that two people are very similar. It applies not only to identical twins but to any two people who share something in common. Two people who love the same type of books and spend a lot of time together discussing books are alike two peas in a pod. This expression is lost on folks who have never shelled field peas or butter beans by hand all day long. Just take the word of someone who knows by experience that peas in the pod are very similar. Although we never call it a pea pod, it was a pea shell or hull. Pea hulls were fed to the cows, but it was felt that butter bean hulls would kill cows. Don't know if it is true; we never tested the folk theory.

An ornery cuss: An ill-tempered, disagreeable individual. "Ah, don't pay that grumpy ole man any mind—he's just an ornery ole cuss."

Ant or Ain't: "Not" or "are not" as in "Yankees ant us!"

Antebellum: Before *the War*—the War for Southern Independence, incorrectly labeled "the *Civil War*" by Yankees and miseducated Southerners.

Aren't you precious: Mostly used by female Southerners as an expression of sarcasm.

As out of place as a red-headed stepchild at the family reunion: Out of place, someone who does not fit in with the group. Sometimes "As mistreated as a red-headed stepchild." Also, "As mistreated as a borrowed mule."

As the crow flies: Measuring distance in a straight line without regard to hills and curves on the road. "It's about 30 miles to Jackson from here, *as the crow flies*." The actual road distance will be slightly more than 30 miles when considering the crooked layout of most country roads back in the day.

At a loss: Not sure or cannot remember the details of an event. "I'm *at a loss* as to where I left my bowl of grits."

Back in the day: In times past. The phrase could mean a few days, months, years, or generations prior. It depends on the context in which it is used. If grandma says, "*Back in the day* we didn't have fancy wood burning stoves, we had to cook over an open fire in the fireplace." You know from the context and the speaker that she is speaking about generations past—not days past.

Barking up the wrong tree: Hunting dogs have a unique and, to a skilled hunter, an easily distinguishable bark when on the trail of game and another distinctive bark when the animal pursued by the dog "goes to tree," i.e., climbs up into a tree to get away from the dogs (treed). The hunter then goes to the sound of the dog barking "treed," and the hunter looks up into the tree to find the game. Sometimes, the game will jump from the first tree to a second tree, and the dog will not see it as it jumps—thus, the dog was *barking up the wrong tree*. As applied to humans, it means that someone who thinks he or she is correct about something, but actually, they are wrong in their assumption. Without realizing it, they are *barking up the wrong tree*. This is true for most Southern historians who dutifully repeat Yankee lies and slander about the reasons we fought the War for Southern Independence.

Beat like a borrowed mule: Used to describ when someone or a loaned item is misused, with little respect for the person or thing misused.

Better off: Having a greater financial or material advantage than another person. The term is also used to indicate any improved condition. "Ole Billy Bob is *better off* now that he gave up hard liquor."

Bible-Belt: Another term for the South or *Dixie*. It consists of the states of the former Confederacy. It is the area of the United States where there are more churches (Protestant and Catholic) per capita than any other region of the United States. The term is used as a pejorative by our detractors but we accept it as an unintended complement to our Christian faith.

Bite off more than you can chew: To take on a task you are unable to complete. The Bible tells us about the man who began to build but did not first count the cost, and therefore, he failed to complete his project—he bit off more than he could chew! During *the War*, Southern soldiers were always hungry and felt lucky to have hardtack to eat. Hardtack is a very hard, thick, cracker. It has the consistency of hard plaster, and it tastes just about as good. If the soldier bit off more than a very small piece, he would not be able to chew it. Most soldiers used their bayonets to break the hardtack into small pieces and boiled several small pieces in their tin coffee cups to make it chewable. Like many Southern sayings, it was probably around before *the War* but became deeply embedded in the language during *the War* and was passed down to successive Southern generations.

Bittie: A baby chicken recently hatched. The word comes from the Celtic word "bit," meaning small. Bit was also a denomination of Spanish money used in early America. A Spanish bit was worth around 12.5 cents. Two bits is equal to 25 cents (a quarter). Most often used today as a football cheer: "Two bits, four bits, six bits, a dollar. All for (team's name) stand up and holler!" Eight bits would equal four quarters which equals a dollar. *Back in the day* it was very common to hear someone refer to a quarter as "two bits."

Bless your heart: Well, bless his heart, or well, bless her heart. Generally said as sarcasm directed toward a sweet but misguided individual who needs to mature or gain more life experience. But it can also be used as a sincere, prayerful expression of solicitation for Divine Blessing toward an individual. It depends upon the speaker's tone of voice. "Did you hear that ole Jim's only mule up and died?" "Oh, no! Well, bless his heart." That blessing would be for Jim, not the dead mule.

Bless your pea-pickin heart: A sincere blessing bestowed upon your social equal. Tennessee Ernie Ford made the expression popular by turning it into a song sung at the close of his TV show back in the 1950s.

Board-and-batten(batting): A type of construction used *back in the day* primarily for out-buildings (barns, sheds, smokehouses, etc.). Planks, eight to twelve inches wide, cut from second grade logs or sap wood would be nailed in place vertically, instead of horizontally as is typically done, and the crack between two adjacent vertical boards is covered by a third vertically nailed board. The third board that covers the crack is about three to four inches wide.

Boot: As in a tire *boot*. A piece of a discarded tire that is cut to fit inside a worn tire that has a hole in the tread. The inflated innertube holds the *boot* in place. Used when a poor man could not afford a new tire.

Bowed up: Ready to fight, or ready for heated confrontation.

Brave as the first man to eat a raw oyster: Said about someone willing to try almost anything.

Britches: Pants. "That boy has gotten too big for his *britches*." More formal folks would use the term "trousers." *Britches* were an essential item of clothing for ancient cavalrymen or for men blazing trails through thick, thorn-infested, thickets and overgrown forests.

Brogans: Short leather boots covering ankles worn by field hands.

Burn the midnight oil: To spend a great deal of time working on a particular project. Teachers often told their failing students to *burn the midnight oil* — meaning the students should study extra hard that night if they expect to pass the next day's test. Back when any studying or reading at night would be done by the light of a *coal-oil* lamp — burning the lamp late in the night required expending of costly coal-oil.

Can't make a silk purse out of a sow's ear: You can't take something rough and uncultured and turn it into something highly rated or valued. It can also be applied to a crude individual who is appointed or elected to a position of honor but who embarrasses those who supported the individual.

Cattywampus: Something is crooked, off-centered, askew.

Caught with your pants down: In the old days (time before around 1965), *field hands* did not have the convenience of porta-potties (portable toilets). When the "call to nature" came, they would "go to the woods" to relieve themselves. If they were not careful in choosing the site, someone might walk upon them and catch them with their pants down. To avoid such embarrassment, it was an informal rule that men went to a given patch of woods and women went to another.

Civil War: The incorrect term for the War for Southern Independence. It is incorrect because a *civil war* is a struggle between two factions in the same country — one trying to capture control of the country and the other trying to maintain its control of the country. When the American Colonies seceded from the British Empire in 1776, it was not a *civil war*; the same holds true for when the Southern States seceded from the United States in 1861. The South was attempting to fulfill the American principle boldly declared in the Declaration of Independence that all people have an inalienable right to establish a government based upon the consent of the governed. And as a Virginia lady once declared, "There was not a darn thing civil about it!" Also, see *The War*.

Coal oil: A form of kerosene. *Coal oil* dates back to ancient times. Before rural electrification, homes and rural churches were lit by the light of *coal oil* lamps. There is a technical/chemical difference between coal oil and kerosene, but the difference is so minor and unnoticeable to the user that kerosene would be referred to as *coal oil* until the late 1960s.

Coke: That wonderful carbonated beverage invented in 1886 by Colonel John Stith Pemberton, formerly of the Confederate Army. When a Southerner says he is going to get a coke, he may return with a root beer or a Dr. Pepper (by the way the inventor of Dr. Pepper was also a former Confederate officer). The brand name *Coke* is often used in the South to signify any carbonated beverage. It is not unusual to hear someone ask, "What kind of coke do you want?" Meaning what particular brand of carbonated beverage do you want. But *Coke* is the real thing in the South. When a Southerner orders a *Coke* in a restaurant and the waitress asks, "Will Pepsi do?" the answer is, "No ma'am, it will not do, but I'll have to take it if that is all you have." It is the same reaction a Southerner has when he orders sweet tea, and the waitress responds, "We don't have sweet tea; I'll bring some sweetener with a glass of unsweetened tea. Will that do?" Bless her heart! She can't help it—she is working at some idiotic Yankee franchise that has no concept of the cultural importance of sweet tea or how to make it! Sometimes, it is hard to be polite. But being *ugly* to the waitress will not improve the situation, and it would be wrong. My response usually is, "I'll just have a *coke*," while silently praying, "Please, God, don't let her ask me if Pepsi will do."

Comeuppance: Punishment finally administered to someone who has avoided justifiable and well-deserved punishment for a long time. "Wow! That bully finally got his *comeuppance* when he tried to push ole Jim Bob around."

Coming up a cloud: Storm clouds on the horizon and headed this way. "You *young'uns* get in this house! Don't you see it's a *coming up a cloud*?"

Commotion: A turmoil, uproar, or disturbance. Same as a *ruckus*. "What's all that *commotion* up there—you *young'uns* settle down and go to sleep!"

Cooking with gas: A vast improvement over prior conditions. If you are *cooking with gas*, you no longer need to cut, split, and stack fire wood for the wood-burning stove.

Coon's age: A long time. "I haven't seen ole Bubba in a *coon's age*."

Corn pone: Corn-bread made from batter using water instead of milk and very little, if any, seasoning. The purpose of *corn pone* was to *make do* with the limited resources available—which is a lesson the impoverished Southern people were forced to learn. *Corn pone* is called the rustic cousin of corn-bread. Some Yankee-authored dictionaries give the first or primary definition of *corn pone* as an adjective describing someone lacking sophistication. Because *corn pone* is almost exclusively a "Southern thang" (thing), it would be reasonable to believe the Yankee authors were talking about poor Southerners. This exemplifies how nonchalantly Yankees treat their continuing slander of Southerners. Ever since they conquered and occupied us, they feel free to mock us and make us the butt of their condescending jokes. As one Southern writer in the 1930s sadly bemoaned, Yankees expect Southerners to remain quietly "upon the everlasting stools of repentance." In Lincoln's newly created supreme federal empire, the South's only purpose is to provide her sons for the nation's military and meekly accept our national role as the target of Yankee jokes and ridicule while serving as the scapegoat for the national sins of slavery and racism. Never forget that slavery existed in every colony when the Colonies seceded from their union with Great Britain in 1776.

And the money (capital) used to create Yankee industrial power came primarily from their active participation in the nefarious international slave trade. Yankee historians prefer that you never know about such inconvenient facts—that is why they write and enforce their version of American history, while censoring efforts of the captive nation to tell its side of the story.

Couldn't carry a tune in a number three zinc bucket: Tone deaf; unable to harmonize.

Cousins: Part of the extended family. Your first cousin would be the child of your mother's or father's brother (your uncle) or sister (your aunt). We generally count cousins down to fifth cousins. It was common for our family to refer to our neighbor, Mr. Mike Guess, as Cousin Mike because he was Dad's second cousin. As usual with Southerners, we shorten "cousin." Instead of saying the formal and correct "Cousin Mike," we would say "Cutten Mike."

Cox's Army: A large gathering of people. "We had enough food at the church's pot-luck *supper* to feed *Cox's Army*." Also: "They made more noise than *Cox's Army*." *Cox's Army* (Coxey is the correct spelling) was a protest march on Washington organized by Jacob Coxey from Ohio in 1894. It was the second year of a four-year depression that produced a dramatic economic downturn in the Northern states. The South was so impoverished that the depression of 1893-96 was hardly noticed. While the North was enjoying the "Gilded Age" and the "Age of Robber Barons," the South was mired in Northern-imposed poverty. The Kennedy Twins explain this in "Punished With Poverty-the Suffering South."

Cracker: A common term used to describe the *plain folk* of the old South. First used in North America by Spanish officials in Florida to describe whites driving their cattle and ox cart using the cracking of bull whips. The first recorded use of the term was in 1595 by William Shakespeare when he asks, "What *cracker* is this same that deafs our ears with abundance of superfluous breath?" (Meaning the individual talks too loud and too much). The English used the term to demean boisterous and loud talking Irish. It has nothing to do with the cracking of whips over slaves as some slanderous, anti-South writers and pundits have asserted.

Croaker sack: A course weave, brown, feed sack. Also, called a jute sack, toe sack, burlap sack, or gunny sack. It is made of inexpensive, coarse, burlap fiber, which comes from jute or hemp plants.

Cultural Distortion: The unnatural corruption of a society that occurs when the natural social relations of a people within a specific culture are radically changed due to the imposition of an outside force. It describes the occurrence of adverse social changes that generally would not have occurred without some unnatural or external force. For example, the cooperation of the French in Vichy France with the Nazi forces during World War II while the Nazis occupied France. Racial segregation and white supremacy laws that occurred in the post-War South are also examples of *cultural distortion*—caused by Yankee invasion and occupation.

Darling, Sugar, Honey, Sweetheart: Terms of endearment. Depending on the tone and speaker, it may be a simple way of saying thank you to a helpful checkout clerk, "Thank you, *sweetheart*, for all your help." Or it could be used in a more romantic form, "*Sweetheart*, God only knows how I got so lucky as to find a beautiful wife like you, but I sure am thankful I did." Whether these words are used as a sincere expression of respect or romantic love can only be determined by the speaker's voice tone and facial expression at the time the words are spoken. This is one of the objections I have for texting and emailing—they are attempts to communicate absent the human element. They are useful tools, but they are not a substitute for human face-to-face communication. By the way, Southerners, especially Southern women, can use these words as a sly form of sarcasm—again, it depends on the context, voice tone, and facial expression.

Darn tooten: Without a doubt—correct as stated. "You're *darn tooten* I'm a rebel!"

Deaf in one ear. and can't hear out of the other: Someone who is hearing impaired. Usually made about oneself "Sorry, I did not hear you. I'm *deaf in one ear, and can't hear out of the other.*"

Deo Vindice: Latin, roughly translated it means: vindication is of God, or God shall vindicate. It is the motto of the Confederate States of America and seen at the end of many pro-South books and articles.

Dinner: The noon meal, typically eaten at home. Workers who carry their noon meal to work using a lunch box or lunch pail etc., eat lunch. Southerners who take time to sit down at noon while at home or a restaurant eat *dinner*. If you are still confused, see *supper*.

Divide and rule: A political technique used by empires that allows the empire to maintain control of an invaded, conquered, and occupied people with the least amount of cost to the empire. The British Empire used *divide and rule* to help them control the population of Scotland and India. The victorious North used it by driving a wedge of mistrust and hatred between black and white Southerners. See details in "Punished With Poverty-the Suffering South."

Dixie: The South consisting of up to 16 states south of the Mason-Dixon Line. *Dixie* is a land of memories. It's a land of beauty, charm, and grace, but most of all it's a land that remembers. *Dixie* was formed in the furnace of war, tested in the crucible of Reconstruction, and she endures intentionally imposed poverty. Those who know and love her call her home and still stand when they hear "Dixie," the South's National Anthem, played. Before *the War*, when men from upriver floated their goods down the Mississippi River to New Orleans, they boasted that they would return with their pockets full of Dixies—the ten-dollar "Dix" note issued by the bank of New Orleans. Soon all the land south of the Ohio River was referred to as Dixieland or *Dixie*.

Don't count your chicks before they hatch: A hen may lay a dozen or more eggs, but all of her eggs may not hatch. Counting the eggs, the hen is "setting" on will not tell you how many chicks you will end up with. (Baby chicks are called *bitties* which is an old *Scotch-Irish* expression meaning baby chicks). *Don't count your chicks until they hatch* is a warning about expectations. For example, we may expect our team to win, but we should save the real celebrating and bragging until after the final score. A lesson Alabama taught LSU many times, but not in 2019!

Don't get your feathers in a ruffle (or *all ruffled up*): Hens with chicks to protect tend to walk around the barnyard with their feathers ruffled, which makes them appear a lot larger than they actually are. If you try to get close to her chicks, the hen will peck you. As used concerning people, it is a plea for someone to settle down, cool down, or calm down. Don't get angry and control your anger.

Don't let your alligator mouth overload your hummingbird behind: Also known as someone with big talk and little action. "Little man, you keep pestering that big ole boy, and he's going to turn on you and give you a good whipping—*your alligator mouth is just about to overload your hummingbird behind.*"

Don't start me to lying: Said when you do not know the answer to a question directed to you. A humorous way of admitting you don't know the answer.

Don't wear out your welcome: Do not overstay your visit. Know when it is time to leave.

Doohicky: An object that you don't know or can't recall what it is called. Other words similarly used would be thingamabob and whatchamacallit.

Draft: Cold air coming through an opening into the room. "I feel a *draft* in this room. Someone check to see if the window is up."

Drag: A bull-whip used to drive oxen or cattle.

Drovers: Men who use bull-whips to guide yokes (teams) of oxen.

Druthers: To prefer one thing over another. "If I had my druthers, I would be back in sweet home Alabama."

Egg on: To encourage or tempt someone — usually to do something they probably should not do. "He would not have gone to the bootlegger's place had his buddies not *egged* him on."

Enough money to burn a wet mule: A reference to someone who has a lot of money. Similar to saying, "He's got money to burn," just sounds more dramatic when you refer to burning a wet mule.

Enough to make a preacher cuss: Something or someone very exasperating or aggravating. Sometimes referred to as something so aggravating, it would cause you to lose your religion. Preachers and good Christians do not cuss, but some things are so bad, it puts a strain on even preachers and good Christians. "Dealing with that highfalutin woman all day long is going to make me lose my religion. Why, she is so opinionated and hardheaded, dealing with her would *make a preacher cuss*."

Even an old blind hog can find an acorn every now and then: Someone who has more luck than good sense. "That boy is not smart; he is just lucky. *Even an old blind hog can find an acorn every now and then*."

Every dog has his day: Everyone gets lucky once in a while. Shakespeare used the saying in Hamlet (Act 5, Scene 1), "The cat will mew, and the dog will have his day." Similar to the expression, "*Even an old blind hog will find an acorn every now and then*."

Extinction theory: Northern belief that blacks would die off after emancipation.

Fandangle: Something new, elaborate, or ornate. Unique but untested. "That's just another *fandangle* Yankee contraption."

Fatback: The fat cut from the hogs back. Belly fat or pork belly is fat with an almost equal amount of meat intertwined. It is the source of bacon. Leaf fat is the purest type of pork fat. It comes from around the kidneys. Lard made from leaf fat is used to make flaky pastries. My Uncle Frank, during hog killing time, gave me these instructions when I was around eight years old.

Fat lighter: Pine-wood used in small pieces to kindle or start a fire. Sometimes referred to as kindling wood, it is used to start (kindle) a fire. Due to its high *rosin* content, fat liter is not used for cooking, because the smoke from the burning pine would give the food the flavor of pine *rosin*. Pine kindling is used to get the fire started and hardwood such as oak, pecan, or hickory is used for cooking the food or heating the house.

Favors: Looks like or resembles someone or thing. "That boy sure favors his uncle." Also used to ask for assistance: "Will you do me a favor?"

Fetch: To go get something and bring it to the requesting individual.

"Fetch" is often used when teaching a dog to bring back a stick or ball thrown by the dog's owner.

Field-hand: Someone who is paid to work a field. A farmer working his own field is not a *field-hand*, although the work he performs is no different. He may refer to his boys and girls who work the field beside him as his field-hands, but technically, they are not actual *field-hands*. A sharecropper working a field on halves or "shares" is a *field-hand*. The land owner provides the land, tools, plow animals, seed, fertilizer, a tenant house, and usually loans the sharecropper money. In return, the land owner keeps half of the produce/crop, and the sharecropper keeps the other half. The sharecropper's share of the crop is his payment for working the land owner's field. *Field-hand* is most often used in the phrase "sweating like a *field-hand*," which acknowledges just how hard life was for all Southerners who worked the fields, but especially for the *field-hands*. Yankees often think of *field-hands* as being strictly black Southerners, but, as usual, when discussing things about the South, Yankees are wrong or perhaps just misguided by their Yankee educational system. Most *field-hands* were sharecroppers, and over 60% of sharecroppers were white Southerners. This is only one of countless examples of how the lies written by Yankee historians and journalists (fake history, fake news, or, in reality, Yankee propaganda) distorted the truth about our South.

Fine as frog hair: An exaggerated way of saying that you feel great or that something is very good. "Split four ways," is added if it is really fine!

Fish or cut bait: Enough talking, either get busy working, or get out of the way of those who will do the work. "Now boys, we've spent enough time a talking about plowing—it's time to *fish or cut bait*." Sometimes, "Fish or go home."

Fit to be tied: Someone who is very angry or upset.

Fixing: Getting ready to do something: "I'm a *fixin'* to go to town." I'm still looking for a good explanation of the origin of this almost exclusively Southern word.

Fly off the handle: A warning to control one's temper because when we say or do things when we are angry, it often causes unintended damage. When chopping wood with an ax, the iron ax head will *fly off* (slip off) *the handle* occasionally, and if it hits someone standing nearby, it could cause a severe injury. The majority of white Southerners are of *Scotch-Irish* (Celtic) descent and are noted for their "hot temper" or "quick temper" and the tendency to fight. This quick temper also means that they tend to do a lot of apologizing. It's best to learn to control your temper and not allow yourself to be easily provoked — don't *fly off the handle*. Note: *Scotch-Irish* (Celtic) peoples were the dominant ethnic group making up the Southern population by 1860. *Scotch-Irish* was not the only group. Of course, African Americans made up the second largest group as well as Germans, French, English, Hispanics, and Native Americans. Southern scholar and historian, Dr. Grady McWhiney, noted that even Germans living in the South tended to take on Celtic cultural traits. Southern culture is a blend of the diverse groups making up our South. While the *Scotch-Irish* culture influenced African American culture, the opposite is also true — African Americans in the South influenced *Scotch-Irish* Southerners. The other ethnic groups in the South also added their influence on our Southern society.

Gave up on: When a person stops a difficult or unprofitable endeavor. To cease making an effort to accomplish a task. "The teacher finally just *gave up on* trying to teach that boy anything."

Gee haw: Commands given by a teamster driving horses or mules or a plowman directing mule or horse as he plows. Gee means go right, and haw means to go left. When used together, talking about someone as in: "We just don't *gee haw*," it means that the two people do not work well together.

Give me a holler: Telling a friend to call you when he needs your help, or you all want to do something together. "*Give me a holler* when you get ready to go coon hunting." Mom and Dad told us of the time when in the quiet of the evening, folks sat on their front porch and talked (tawked as we would say) to their neighbors down the road with ease. They would "give a holler" to get their neighbor's attention and carry on an otherwise normal conversation. This was before TV, radio, telephones, air conditioning, or even electric lights — no noise pollution.

Going hog wild: Similar to "going whole hog" but usually in reference to having fun, perhaps drinking too much adult beverage, or driving too fast. "Jim Bob went *hog wild* running his four-wheeler through the mud holes down at the creek."

Going off half-cocked: To *go off half-cocked* is an expression dating back to the days of muzzleloading black powder rifles. During the War for Southern Independence, it became a matter of life or death. When you load your weapon, the first step is to place black powder and a Minié ball in the barrel and ram it home with the ramrod. You then half-cock the hammer, remove the spent percussion cap, and place a new cap on the firing nipple. If you are firing on the beat of the drum or firing at the enemy (Yankees) at will, then you pull the hammer back to full cock, take aim, and fire. But if you are ordered to load and move to another position, you do not leave your weapon on half-cock — you gently lower the gun's hammer onto the percussion cap before you begin to move to the new position. Otherwise, with the hammer in half-cock position, the percussion cap could fall off the firing nipple. If you need to fire your gun in a hurry, you will cock it without looking at the firing nipple (a Yankee may be getting ready to shoot you—you are in a hurry), and when you pull the trigger, all you hear is the click of metal on metal. Your percussion cap fell off the gun's firing nipple while you were moving to the new position, and you are now facing the enemy who did not *go off half-cocked*! Never *go off halfcocked*! Today, it means to start a project without having all the facts or a good plan to complete the project.

Going to bed with the chickens: Going to bed at or shortly after sundown. We used to say that Uncle Frank *goes to bed with the chickens*. What we meant was that he went to bed shortly after sun down. Chickens go to roost as soon as it starts to gets dark—thus, the term *goes to bed with the chickens*, or he goes to bed about the same time as the chickens go to roost—or simply goes to bed early at night.

Going whole hog: *Going whole hog* is a term meaning that the individual put all he had into an effort. "When it came time for the chitterling eating contest that ole boy went *whole hog* and won!" Note: Chitterlings are pronounced as chitlins. Just one more word Southerners tend to shorten. Yankees think we are mispronouncing it, but our pronouncement is correct when used within the culture of Southern American English. It seems that I'm *going hog wild* on this topic.

Gone back on his raisin: To betray or turn away from the way in which you were raised, or to deny your heritage. Most modern-day Southern history professors have *gone back on their raisin*. It indicates a betrayal of one's own people and culture in exchange for material gain. The Bible story of Esau (Genesis 25:29-34) is an example; Esau sold his birthright for a bowl of porridge (soup). *Going back on your raisin* occurs today when Southerners trade their spiritual heritage in exchange for fleeting material pleasures or an attempt to be accepted in America's secular humanist, politically correct, materialistic society.

Goober peas: Peanuts. "The Georgia militia, eating *goober peas*."

Good don't pull bad up, but bad will always pull good down: A warning given by Southern mothers to their children. Similar to other warnings often cited by Southern mothers, "You are known by the company you keep," or "If you lie down with dogs, you will get up with fleas."

Good intentions: Southern mothers often remind their children that, "The road to hell is paved with *good intentions*." There are many unforeseen consequences to a given action. Contemporary social justice warriors may have *good intentions*, but their acts and socialist programs have the potential for pernicious results.

Good Lord willing and the creek don't rise: A commitment to do something if nothing very unusual happens to prevent or hinder the individual from completing the commitment. The phrase "Good Lord willing" is a simple statement that nothing will be done if God decides to prevent it. The phrase "if the creek don't rise" *harkens back* (goes back) to the days before good roads and bridges. During a flash flood or just a hard rain, the creek will "rise" or overflow its banks. Many country roads did not have bridges across small creeks. You had to cross the creek at the ford, which is a place where the water runs across the road as a shallow but wide flow of water. This means that you can't cross a creek during a flood. Even wooden bridges may be washed out, but in either case, you will not be able to travel to your destination. Barring any such natural events — you are committing to do something. In the South, your word is your bond — honor requires that you keep your word. Note: The word "harkens" is from the New Testament, "Harken unto me every one of you..." Mark 7:14 and literally means to listen. But when used by Southerners in the phrase *harkens back*, it means to go back in time.

Good ole boy: A fun-loving, easy-going Southern male — applied without regard to his age or race. The term was made popular by the 1970s TV series Dukes of Hazard's opening song describing the young men as "just good ole boys, never meaning no harm." I'm not sure what the double negative implies!

Got to give the Devil his dues: Recognizing that even evil people can be successful in their immoral endeavors. "He is good at being bad." The saying is often used to give credit to someone you don't particularly like, such as, a personal opponent who is successful at some legitimate activity.

Grub stake: A term used mainly out west to describe the financing of a solitary prospector by the general store. The prospector agrees to share a portion of any gold or silver he finds in return for the store providing him with supplies. Similar to the way a Southern landowner provided supplies and equipment to the landless sharecropper. In return, the sharecropper would be allowed a percentage (a share) of the crop he produces, while the landowner keeps the balance. Unlike the solitary prospector, the sharecropper had an entire family to support.

Haints: Haints are goblins and ghosts and other creatures from beyond the grave. Superstitious Southerners (black and white) believed that before a *haint* could come into your house, it must first go into every bottle on your blue-bottle tree. Warning: this only works for blue bottles. If the *haint* completes the trip through every blue bottle before sunrise, he can then enter the house and "haintify" (the act of a spirit haunting a house) the living in the house. But if the homeowner took the additional precaution of placing classified ads from several newspapers on the wall, then the *haint*, upon entering the house, must read every word of newsprint before sunrise. After reading all the newsprint, it can then begin haintifying the folks in the house. To be especially secure from *haints*, the homeowner could go down to French-speaking Cajun Louisiana and purchase Cajun-French language classified ads. Very few *haints* could read French! Today, many Southerners place blue-bottle trees in their yards as decorations, and celebration of a by-gone era not because they are superstitious — but who can tell for sure. Better safe than sorry.

Hankerin (Hankering): A longing or craving for something. "I have a *hankerin* for some Sweet Daddy's Barbeque."

Happy (contented) as a fat pig in a mud hole: One who knows how to enjoy the leisure of the moment without concern about worldly affairs. Hogs do not sweat, to keep cool during hot Southern days, they find a mud hole to wallow in. The expression has been used often in reference to the Southern emphasis on leisure time as opposed to the Yankee stress on productive economic activity, i.e., working to make more money. It has been said often that Yankees live to work while Southerners work to live. Another way of distinguishing Yankees and Southerners is the old saying that "A Yankee will not eat anything he can sell, while the Southerner will not sell anything he can eat." The unique cultural difference between Northerners and Southerners has been around since Europeans first came to North America. The Kennedy Twins discuss the North/South cultural differences in chapter one of "Yankee Empire: Aggressive Abroad and Despotic at Home."

Harken back: Harken is an old English word meaning to pay attention to a given subject. To *harken back* is to remember or take note of something that came before.

Hardheaded: Stubborn. "That ole boy is so *hardheaded* that he has to butt with his own head just to find out that a brick wall is solid."

Head off: A direction of travel. "You need to *head off* home now, boy. Don't you see it's a *coming up a cloud*?"

Hear tell: An admission that one's information is second hand. "I hear tell the church is getting a new preacher."

Heavens to Betsy: A good natured way to express surprise or being astounded upon seeing or hearing about something.

He sows his wild oats on Saturday night and goes to church Sunday praying for a crop failure: A warning that praying after the fact will not necessarily spare you from the earthly consequences of prior bad choices.

He's an egg-sucking dawg (dog): He is no good, does more damage than good, not someone you would trust. Hound dogs and watch dogs are useful to have on the farm. But occasionally, a dog will learn to eat eggs and get to them before the farmer's wife can gather the eggs. Such dawgs have a short life expectancy on a working farm.

He's so fat, it would take at least two dawgs to bark at him: Referring to someone grossly overweight.

Heap: A pile or a large amount of something. "You sho' (sure) got a *heap* of collard greens thar (there), Ma." When harvesting corn, we would put the ears of corn in *heaps* every twenty to thirty feet along three adjacent rows.

Hear tell: Been told something. "I hear tell that *the South shall rise again!"*

Hew it to the line, and let the chips fall where they may: Tell the truth about a particular issue or set of circumstances regardless of who it may embarrass or make angry. Hewing a log is how early settlers turned logs into construction timbers. A straight line was scored on the log, and the settler used a special type of hewing ax that has an offset or slightly curved handle to turn the round log into a square timber. The curved ax handle allowed the ax man to stand on the log while chopping with less chance of chopping his foot. When you hew the logs the wood chips fly in every direction. The chips will not be particular about who they hit.

Highfalutin: A false sense of high social status. Individuals with an unrealistic high opinion of themselves. "That girl is so *highfalutin.* She thinks all the men want to marry her!" Or as my Aunt Lilly Cole (Berry) Holifield would say, "I wish I could buy her for what she is worth and sell her for what she thinks she is worth."

Hoe: An instrument, hand tool, used by farmers to remove weeds. Two basic types, the older, heaver grub *hoe* and the newer lighter gooseneck *hoe.*

Hoecake: A small amount of corn-bread batter baked out of doors over an open fire. The batter may be normal corn-bread batter or *corn pone* batter. Some folks claim the name came from slaves who were working the cotton field, and at noon, they cooked corn-bread on hoes. Folks who make such claims must have never attempted the feat! I tried it and can tell you that it is *might near* impossible. I quickly discovered at least two problems: (1) because of the angle of the hoe blade, to keep the batter from falling off the hoe blade you have to stand next to the fire (in the middle of the hot Southern summer), and (2) you would have to hold the hoe handle directly above the fire which means your arm, hand, and fingers are also cooking! It might be possible with a certain type of older hoe (grub hoe) to remove the blade from its handle and then use the flat iron blade as a griddle. I think that would be rather impractical because keeping a tight connection between the hoe blade and the handle is very important when hoeing. It is also possible that the section boss would keep one or two worn-out hoe blades to use at noon as a griddle to cook hoe cakes. I'm not saying it was never done, but I have never read of it being done.

Hold your horses: Telling someone to wait patiently. During *the War*, one man out of five in a cavalry unit was detailed to hold horses for the other four cavalrymen when they were required to dismount to engage the enemy (Yankees). If you are the fifth man, your job is to be patient and hold the horses, so the other men would have mounts (horses) if they needed to make a hasty withdrawal or give chase to retreating Yankees.

Holler: The small depression or gully between two hills. It is a colloquialism for hollow. It can also mean to yell or shout out, "Give me a *holler* if you need help."

Hominy: A traditional corn-based food produced by soaking dried corn kernels in lye water and then cooking the puffed corn kernels. Add Tony's Chachere's Creole Seasoning and a little Tabasco—good eating!

Hook, line, and sinker: Being completely fooled by someone or something. When pole fishing, you put bait (usually a worm or cricket) on a hook, the hook is tied to a strong string (the line), and to make the bait sink, you attach a weight (the sinker). An over-enthusiastic and hungry fish will not only take the bait on the hook but grab the line and sinker— he is caught with little hope of breaking free. Applied to a person, it means someone who completely fell for a practical joke, or it could also be used to describe someone who was given false information which he relied upon without question, and it worked out to his disadvantage. People who vote for politicians who promise low taxes while also promising numerous "free" programs and projects are falling for political lies *hook, line and sinker*. There is no such thing as a free lunch.

Hush my mouth (sometimes shut my or your mouth): Used to express amazement or shock upon hearing some unexpected news—often mere gossip. [Gossip] "Did you hear that the preacher's son was seen buying beer at the bootleggers?" [Response] "Well, *hush my mouth!*" It can also be used to indicate appreciation for being told important or interesting news or when someone tells you something amazing: "Did you know that the town drunk got religion and joined the church last Sunday?" "Well, *hush your mouth!*"

Hush up: Be quiet. It is not as offensive as saying "shut up."

I Suwannee (S'wanee): Bible-Belt way of swearing.

If a frog had wings, he wouldn't bump his butt when he jumps the creek: Said to someone when he is lamenting his failure to do or not do something "If I had done *thus and such,*" or "If I had not done *thus and such.*" "If" is a dangerous two letter word.

In a coon's age: Racoons are referred to in the South as "coons." There is no logic to the term *in a coon's age,* but when used by a Southerner, it means a long time, such as: "It's been *a coon's age* since I've had a mess of greens." Note the Southern tendency to shorten words: Racoon becomes coon. Another example is Opossum which becomes possum. It is another oddity of Southern American English — even though we tend to speak slowly and therefore, would have plenty of time to use full words; we still tend to shorten some words. It may be the impact the black (slave) dialect had on white Southern speech.

In high cotton: Easy living, the good life, no hard work required. It comes from the fact that picking cotton that is "low cotton" requires bending over (stoop labor) all day in the hot Southern sun, whereas you can stand up straight or at least not bend over as far while picking "high" or tall cotton. Cotton will grow "low" during a drought or when the rain fell well after the cotton began putting on cotton bolls. If rain-fall occurs shortly after the cotton is *laid by,* it will grow tall and produce much better. I've picked both and can tell you that picking high cotton is much better than picking low cotton. Today, cotton is picked mechanically with the tractor driver sitting inside an air conditioned cab. Mechanically picked cotton leaves a small amount of cotton on the cotton plant as "scraps." *Back in the day,* sharecroppers went back into the field after the initial hand picking was done and picked the "scrap" cotton in an effort to gain all the possible value from their crop.

In short order: A short period of time.

Jim Crow: A reference to laws requiring racial segregation passed in the late 1890s, mainly in Southern states — de jure (by law) racial segregation. In the North, where there was a small number of blacks relative to the white Northern population, racial segregation was enforced by custom — de facto (as a matter of custom) racial segregation. Jim Crow laws were not necessary in the North, but racial segregation still existed in the North. Pre-War Northern travelers in the South often complained that down South, black and white folks traveled together, ate together, and were generally very close to each other. This shocked the racial sensitivities of white Northerners. President John Adams (from New England) wrote that among the reasons the Northern people wanted to end slavery were that Northern whites did not want to compete against black craftsmen, and white Northerners generally disliked or hated blacks — they were not too happy about the

Irish either! The segregation law that the U.S. Supreme Court used in 1896 as a precedent to give racial segregation Federal legal sanction was an 1846 law enacted by the legislature of the Yankee state of Massachusetts. When it comes to racial segregation, there is enough guilt to go around, but those who hold the power of the Federal government and their "intellectual" sycophants have managed to avoid their share of guilt. These Yankee "intellectuals" and their scallywag toadies have used their power to turn the defeated and defenseless South into their scapegoat. (A scapegoat is an innocent party who is forced to take the blame for the wrongs of another party. The concept of a scapegoat comes from the Old Testament tradition in which the High Priest ceremonially placed the sins of the nation on the head of a goat and sent the goat out to die in the wilderness.)

Just as busy as a stump-tailed cow in fly time: Someone who is very busy. This saying is lost on city folks. Milk does not come from the milk factory—it comes from cows that must be milked every day. In the old days, dairy farmers milked their cows by hand. One of the first "grown-up" tasks Donald and I learned when we were around nine years old was how to milk a cow. Each land-owning family had one or two cows that provided the family with milk. To milk the cow, you must sit close to the ground near the cow's hind legs. Milking one cow by hand takes around 15 to 20 minutes. During the summer when biting flies are worse, the cow will use her long tail to shue (also spelled shoo) the flies off her back. (As in the song "Shue Fly Shue Don't You Bother Me"). If the cow has lost her tail—stump-tailed, she has no way to defend herself from biting flies except to swing her head back over her front shoulder in a futile attempt to shue the flies away. Thus, she is as busy as a stump-tailed cow in fly time.

Katy bar the door: Get ready; there's trouble a-coming. "Be careful boy! You get that Clampett clan stirred-up (angry), and it will be Katy bar the door when you see those Clampett boys a-coming." Some folks think this saying comes from an old Scottish folk-song "Get Up and Bar the Door" that was brought to American by the *Scotch-Irish*. I have also heard it expressed as "Katy bar the door; here comes the Indians." This would certainly agree with the *Scotch-Irish* settlement of the Southern backcountry populated with numerous Native Americans who were not happy to see white settlers coming into their tribal land. This causes me to think about the old expression: "All land is sword land." It means that land is won by the sword (irregular or regular military force); all land is kept by the sword. It is a sad fact of human history that whenever a people get soft, they will become easy prey for a more vigorous people who will dispossess them of their homeland. As written in one version of "Scotland the Brave," "Freedom dies amid softness and sighs."

Keep: To remain useful for its intended purpose. *Sweet milk* would *keep* for only a short time before it soure — in the era before refrigeration.

Keep soul and body together: Efforts necessary to survive. This was a very common expression in the post-War, impoverished, South. Before *the War*, the South was the wealthiest section of the United States, consuming and exporting large quantities of food stuff. After *the War*, the South became a net importer of food, with a large number of the population malnourished and many succumbing to disease and starvation. The whole family had to work from can, to can't (sun up to sun down) just to *scratch out a living*. Otherwise, it would not be possible to *"keep soul and body together."* The Kennedy Twins explain this in "Punished With Poverty-the Suffering South."

Keep your lamps trimmed: To pay attention to the small details that make life easier or prevent small problems from becoming large problems. It comes from the time *back in the day* when the only light available in the house after sundown was light from *coal-oil* lamps. The wick on these lamps must be trimmed occasionally. Failure to do so will cause the wick to burn and smoke-up the lamp's globe and the entire house.

Kith and kin: An old *Scotch-Irish* term meaning friends, neighbors, and those related by blood. By custom, *kith and kin* are honor-bound to come to the aid of each other in times of distress or danger. It is a natural part of a people who have a high sense of community and a people who believe in and practice the idea that we have a Christian duty to "help your fellow man."

Knee-high to a grasshopper: A reference to a young child. "I haven't seen her since she was *knee-high to a grasshopper*."

Laid-by or *Lay-by:* A farming technique used as the final plowing of a crop. After the crop is *laid-by*, the farmer has four to six weeks before the crops mature and will be ready for harvesting.

Lagniappe: A Louisiana Cajun French word expressing something given over and above what was due and owing, or expected. A bonus or special gift given to express appreciation. The old expression of a baker's dozen is similar. *Back in the day* when you ordered a dozen doughnuts, the baker would include a thirteenth doughnut, or a few doughnut holes.

Larapin: Good-tasting food. "We had a fine sardine *larapin* last night."

Lickety-split: Fast: see *skedaddle*.

Liter, fat liter: Pine wood used in small pieces to kindle or start a fire. Sometimes referred to as kindling wood, used to start (kindle) a fire. Due to its high *rosin* content, fat liter is not used to cook with because the smoke from the burning pine would give the food the flavor of pine *rosin*. Pine kindling is used to get the fire started, and hardwood such as oak, pecan, or hickory is used to cook the food or heat the house.

Little-bitty: Something very small. "I'm on a diet so give me a little-bitty piece of mama's peanut brittle." Young chicks newly hatched are called bitties.

Load the wagon boys, don't worry about the mules, just load the wagon: To pile the work on someone without regard to how much effort it will take for the individual to complete the task. I can still hear Uncle Frank telling us this when we were down in the bottomland loading the mule-wagon with fire wood.

Loafers' bench: Bench(es) placed outside the general store, next to the door. Men who had nothing particular to do often sat on the loafers' bench and visited with folks as they entered the store.

Lord have mercy: Usually, but not always, used as a sincere plea for God's intervention for someone. "*Lord have mercy*! That boy is going to kill himself driving like that."

Low peck hen: Chickens have a pecking order from the dominant hen down to the one at the bottom of the order. All the chickens can peck any other chicken lower than itself. The low peck hen is pecked by all the other hens but cannot peck on any other hen—thus the low peck hen. (See: *The pecking order*).

Lunch: There ant no such thing down South. It is something Yankees eat in a rush, while folks down South are sitting with their family, and enjoying *dinner*.

Ma'am and *Sir:* As in yes ma'am, no ma'am etc. A simple act of social grace and civility that helps to maintain a peaceful society. It is an indication of respect. *Back in the day* when men went around armed, it was necessary to speak slowly and respectfully to avoid violent confrontations—this is a major part of our Southern *Scotch-Irish* heritage. These phrases are used not just by Southern children but by adults when speaking to someone older, someone in authority, or a stranger. I can't tell you the number of times I was accosted by a Yankee during a radio interview because I dared to say, "Yes ma'am" when responding to the Yankee. "Don't you ma'am me!" they complained. Without thinking, my polite response was a simple, "Yes ma'am." The Yankee wench would then throw a *hissy fit*.

Make a crop: A Southern term describing the entire process of purchasing supplies, cultivating, planting, fertilizing, plowing, and harvesting a crop.

Make do: To survive on what you have.

Making a living: Working to gain the necessities of life: food, shelter, and clothing. It *harkens back* to the pronouncement of God to fallen mankind in the Garden of Eden: "In the sweat of thy face shalt thou eat bread, till thou return unto the ground," Genesis 3:19.

Mend your fences: To settle a disagreement with a friend, neighbor, or family member in a manner that is mutually agreeable to all parties. There is an old expression that says: "good fences make for good neighbors." Fence lines were very important because they marked off the boundary between one person's land and his neighbor's land. Thus, if the fence line is in question or dispute, then the neighbor's property rights and your property rights will be in question. If you and your neighbor mend the fence separating your property, then you have reconciled the property line between your land and your neighbor's land. It generally means to settle a conflict in a mutually agreeable manner.

Might does not make right: Evil may overpower good but that does not change the nature of evil. Truth, civility, and moral values are <u>not</u> guaranteed victory as the world evaluates victory but honorable men and women will stand by such virtues (truth, civility and morality) even though evil, at the moment, seems to be unstoppable. The Irish were under English domination for centuries, yet the mere passage of time did not legalize or justify English rule of Ireland.

Might near or *might nigh*: Almost or nearly. "I know that cooking *hoecakes* over an open fire using the hoe blade is *might near* impossible."

Milch cow: An old and correct term for a cow held for the purpose of providing milk—a dairy cow. Most folks use the incorrect term "milk cow" which indicates the cow is made of milk—such as a clay cow, a wooden cow, or a milk cow. Donald and I ran across the term *milch cow* when reading the speeches of 1830-40 Southern members of Congress who complained about the North using its majority vote in Congress to extract tariffs from the South. They pointed out that the North was forcing the South to pay 75% of the revenues necessary to run the Federal government. They complained that the North turned the South into "the *milch cow* of the Union." As used by Southern Congressmen, it meant the same as the modern term "cash cow."

More than I can say grace over: An individual who has more work, assignments, or projects than he can handle. In the Bible-Belt South, it is traditional to offer a prayer of thanks for food—say grace or say the Blessing—before eating. If you have more on your plate than you can say grace over, then you have too much or more than you can eat on your plate.

More than one way to skin a cat: Most problems have more than one solution—select the right one. I have also heard it said, "there are more ways to choke a cat than just on butter." This is a good example of a Southernism that combines good advice (many possible solutions usually available) with an outrageous image (choking a cat on butter).

My eyeballs are floating: When you have had your fill of liquid refreshment. "I've drunk so much sweet tea that my eyeballs are floating!" An expression used to express the fact that you have been "over served" or have had all the liquid refreshment you can hold.

No axe to grind or *no dog in the fight*: Having no intrinsic reason to take sides in a discussion or argument. Someone with "no ax to grind" or "no dog in the fight" would make a good neutral party to help settle the dispute because they have no strong opinion one way or the other. These expressions can also be used by an individual who does not wish to be involved in the argument.

No such thing as a free lunch: Everything of material value has a cost. While you may get something "free," it is not without cost — someone paid for what you got "free." The folks in the Bible-Belt understand this from a spiritual sense. Redemption and salvation are free to the sinner who believes in Jesus Christ, but that "free" salvation cost God His Only Begotten Son. It cost Jesus his life on the cross. Someone always has to pay. Politicians often offer free this or free that to certain groups as a way to purchase their votes — legalized vote buying. But all those free programs must be paid for by taxpayers. It is a very convenient political scam by which politicians use taxpayers' money to reward the politician's constituency for voting for the politician. It is a form of vote buying.

Not close anymore: Used in reference to a former friend who, for some reason, you no longer consider a friend or a relative who has embarrassed the family. When someone asks you about the individual, you reply, "We *are not close anymore.*" That response from you not only informs the inquirer that you have no recent information about the individual, but all further questions or discussion about the individual should cease.

Not the sharpest tool in the shed: A polite way of saying that someone is not the smartest one in a group or the individual is lacking common sense.

Nothing good ever comes cheaply: Success is not a gift from the gods. Hard work gives a thing its value. Thomas Pain wrote, "What we obtain too cheap, we esteem too lightly: it is dearness only that gives everything its value."

Okree: Southern pronunciation of okra. Okra is the English word for gumbo, which was brought to North America by African slaves. Today gumbo is the word for a delicious Cajun dish made with okra, seafood and Cajun seasoning. But remember, to make a gumbo, "first you have to make a roux."

Once burned, twice warned: Learning by sad experience—some folks just won't (will not) listen to sound advice and have to find out the hard way.

Out of kilter: Not functioning correct, but has not yet reached the state of being *tore-up*.

Pellagra: A disease that afflicted the people of the South after the end of *the War* and up to the early 1950s. Millions of Southerners suffered from *pellagra*. It is caused by a diet deficient in the vitamin niacin (B 3). It caused the death of over 100,000 black and white Southerners. The Federal government took no significant action to alleviate this post-War suffering caused by this South-only disease. Malnutrition of the local population is a common occurrence after empires invade, conquer, and exploit a formerly free people.

People: As in your *people*, meaning your kinfolk. "Where you from, boy? You have any *people* around here?" The idea being that you can get a good idea of what kind of person someone is if you know their *people*. Family trees are important in judging an individual because "the apple does not fall far from the tree." This is a good general rule, but we always keep in mind that there are both positive and negative exceptions to general rules.

Piddling: Killing time or doing nothing in-particular. "Zeb was just *piddling* around on the *loafers' bench*, whittling big sticks into little sticks."

Pig in a poke: To pay good money for something you have not inspected or take advice from someone who may not be honest. A poke is a paper bag.

Piney woods rooter: A free-ranging hog. *Back in the day* hogs were allowed to roam the open range (vast areas of Southern woodland that no one owned). Once a year, the local community got together and rounded up the hogs. The ownership was determined by the ear notching that was placed on the hogs in the prior year. Young pigs would be caught as they followed their mother and an appropriate ear notch was applied.

Pitcher: Yankees sometimes think we are talking about the baseball player who throws the ball toward the batter. No, this is much more important—it is the container with a spout and pouring handle that usually contains sweet tea. "Mom! We need another pitcher of sweet tea—please." Be careful, if you don't include the "please," you may end up wearing that pitcher of sweet tea! Please and thank you ranks right up there with yes ma'am and no ma'am in the Southern mother's Southern American English dictionary—which she has memorized word for word.

Plain Folk: Plain folk of the old South is a term used to describe the non-plantation white population of the pre-War South. Most *plain folk* did not own slaves. The few who did own slaves owned only one to two families. Both white (*plain folk*) and black (slave) families lived close together and worked the fields together. This close relationship between the races offended whites in the North, but it developed into a close *kith and kin* relationship down South. *Plain folk* were primarily Scotch-Irish whose ancestors brought to the American South the Celtic herding tradition. *Plain folk* families ran thousands of hogs and beef cattle on the South's pre-War open range. As a group, they valued leisure, outdoor activities such as hunting, fishing, and horse racing. Northern writers often mislabeled them as *poor white trash (PWT)*. But in fact, they were a non-materialistic people whose herds in 1860 had a dollar value greater than the combined value of all cotton, tobacco, and rice grown on the South's plantations in 1860.

Playing possum: Pretending to be sleeping or not hearing someone who is calling. "Pour some cold water on that boy—he ant a-sleep—he's just *playing possum*." When attacked, a possum will pretend to be dead. They go into something similar to a catatonic seizure (rigid body posture). Opossum is the correct spelling for the North American animal—possums are found in Australia. There is a difference: two different animals, but by convention, we say possum, and everyone understands that we mean opossum.

Plow-lines: The reins used to control a mule or horse while plowing. Most *plow-lines* were made of cotton rope. Leather reins could be used, but they tended to be more expensive and too heavy to manage all day long while also handling (steering) the plow. A well-trained mule requires very little "steering," while the plow must be manhandled, controlling the direction of the plow point up, down, right, or left, or else you will end up plowing up your crop or just skidding along on top of the ground. While manhandling the plow, the farmer must also calculate whether the plow is throwing too much or too little soil. These *field hands* are the men that secular humanists, neo-Marxists and feminists claim are/were a part of the male patriarchy, who enjoyed unearned male privilege. Privilege?

Plumb: Completely, thoroughly, or totally. "I'm *plumb* tuckered out from all that shopping." By the way: "tuckered out" means exhausted.

Politicians: Folks who make their living telling voters how good they (the *politician*) are and how bad their political opponents are. There is an old Southern saying that, "*Politicians* are like cock-roaches. It's not what they steal and carry off that makes them so bad—it's what they fall into and mess up."

Poor white trash (PWT): The correct usages of the term are a reference to whites who were not a part of the community; living a life not in keeping with Christian teachings; living a life of degradation; and exhibiting low standards of civility. Yankees often incorrectly used the term to refer to non-plantation white Southerners—see *plain folk*.

Pot calling the kettle black: When one person accuses another of a crime or sin of which he or she is also guilty. *Back in the day* of wood burning stoves, cast iron pots and kettles turned black from the smoke. The pot was just a black as the kettle.

Poultice: A home remedy composed of locally available plants and herbs; made into a paste; applied to the injured or swollen part of the body and kept in place with a cloth. By the early 1900s, it was common to apply "store-bought" salve and keep it warm by putting a cloth over the body part to which the salve was applied. It was a common treatment for a chest cold. I have received many an application of Vicks Vapor Rub from Mom while fighting off a chest cold. Also, when the Vicks cobalt blue bottles were empty, they could be cleaned and left next to the bed just in case a *haunt* managed to make it past your blue bottle tree.

Pretty as a little ole speckle puppy! Someone, usually a small child, who is cute or adorable. "Why, that little baby-girl (said as if it is one word) is just as *pretty as a little ole speckle puppy*."

Pretty is as pretty does: A warning given by Southern mothers to their son when he is considering a woman to marry. Regardless of how lovely a person is on the outside (their physical appearance), they may be very *ugly* on the inside. It is typically applied to only females but the same holds true for males. Perhaps: Handsome is as handsome does.

Raise that winder down: Or in modern times: would *yawl* turn the air conditioner's thermometer down? It's getting too cold in here. There is no explaining—it is something many of us say when we want someone to lower a window ("raise it down) or to raise the degree setting on the air conditioner (turn the air conditioner down—make it put out less cold air). In the South, there are some things you don't explain or question; you just accept them.

Rank and file: Originally a military term used during the Napoleonic era to describe soldiers standing in line of battle. Rank (front) would be the line of soldiers standing shoulder to shoulder, then another line (rear rank) standing directly behind the first rank. The man in front and the soldier directly behind him (the soldier to the rear soldier's front) make up the file. As commonly used today, it means the totality of people being discussed.

Rat cheer: Directions to another person on where to put something. "Put that bowl of boiled peanuts *rat cheer* in front of me. I'll take care of 'em!" If something is not over *yonder*, it might be *rat cheer*.

Reckon: To think or surmise. "She is as sweet as a Georgia peach!" "I *reckon* so."

Redneck: A white Southerner. It is often used as a derogatory term by folks who do not understand the South. Some claim that the term came from the hot sun burning the back of a poor white farmer's neck. Some scholars have noted that the term comes from Scotts who refused to abandon their Calvinist faith by joining, under duress, the Church of England. They signed an oath of loyalty to their faith using their blood as ink and wore a red kerchief around their necks as a sign to all of their resistance to English tyranny and were referred to as rednecks. Scottish immigrants brought the term to the South.

Rile, as in all riled-up: To agitate, upset or make someone angry.

Rode hard and put up wet: When someone has been "done wrong" or mistreated. You never put up a hot and sweating horse after a hard ride. You are supposed to walk the horse, allowing it to "blow" (catch its breath) until it cools down and brush it before you put it in the horse barn. To say that someone was *rode hard and put up wet* is to imply that a superior has mistreated him.

Root hog or die: Depend on yourself, don't look to others to supply your needs. It is the unacknowledged motto of people who value their personal liberty based upon self-reliance. It does not contemplate life without help from *your kith and kin,* but such help is mutually given and received. It can also be used as an expression of not caring about the hungry and destitute—*the deserving poor*. Shortly before the end of *the War,* it was pointed out to Yankee President Lincoln that for generations, slaves obtained their food, shelter, and clothing from their plantation. When Lincoln was asked what would the freed slaves do for the necessities of life once the plantation system is destroyed, Lincoln callously replied with a story about a man who said he would not feed his hogs, "they would have to *root hog or die.*" As far as Lincoln was concerned, blacks would have to *root hog or die*. See: *Extinction theory*.

Rosin: The solid form of resin obtained from pine trees. The sap of the pine tree (resin) is very sticky. When cutting pulpwood with a crosscut saw, the saw blade will stick or jam if *coal oil* is not applied to the blade while cutting pine trees. *Rosin* is a key element in *fat litter*. The liquid form is called resin. The ancients called *rosin* Greek pitch.

Rot-gut: Bad whiskey made in secret in a less than safe whiskey still. During the era of prohibition (1920-1933) when alcohol was outlawed in the United States, whiskey was occasionally made covertly using metal pipes and tubes with high lead content, which eventually will poison anyone drinking it.

Ruckus, as in, "to raise a ruckus": To create a great noise or commotion. The ruckus or loud noise is usually not associated with productive activity.

Scalawag: A native Southerner who betrays his Southern heritage in exchange for acceptance by the Yankee establishment and/or financial profit.

Scarce as hen's teeth: Chickens and other birds do not have teeth. They don't chew their food; they have gizzards that grind the food they swallow before it goes to their stomach. Thus, when something is *scarce as hen's teeth*, it does not exist. A tyrant's love for his oppressed people is as *scarce as hen's teeth*.

Scratch out a living: Working hard just to survive. Free ranging chickens scratch the ground to find food to eat. Similar to *keep soul and body together*.

Scotch-Irish: A term used to identify early settlers who came from Northern Ireland and settled in the South, the Ohio Valley, and the Pennsylvania back country. They were Scotts who the English moved to Northern Ireland in an effort to control the rebellious Irish. Eventually, the English oppressed the Scotts as well, and a great migration from Northern Ireland to the South began in the late 1600s.

Short end of the stick: Unlucky or mistreated by his peers. Drawing straws is a way of selecting by lot the person who will be appointed to do a difficult or unpleasant task. "Well, Bubba, you got the *short end of the stick*, so you get to clean the outhouse this week." In conversation, it could be used to indicate that an individual was mistreated, cheated, or simply unlucky. I have also heard "dirty end of the stick."

Show nuff: A positive affirmation regarding the authenticity of another person's statement or to stress the reality of your statement. "The preacher *show nuff* told the truth about the sins of Sodom and Gomorrah."

Shuck: To remove the leaf covering from ears of corn. "Y'all *shuck* the corn and I'll shell it (remove the corn kernels from the corn cob)." Also used as an exclamation. "Ah, *shucks*! Alabama beat Ole Miss again!"

Sight for sore eyes: An expression meaning that you are excited to see someone, most likely someone you have not seen for a *coon's age*.

Single-tree: A wooden rod around two inches in diameter and 18 to 24 inches long with three metal hitch points attached — one on each end and one in the middle. It is used to connect two trace chains to the plow. Also used to hang slaughtered hogs by their hind legs while processing the carcass.

Sister: The oldest girl in the family. When the younger children are infants and toddlers, Sister would be mom's main helper. As the infants and toddlers got older, it was a given fact that Sister was second only to mom when it came to correcting the younger ones and other household affairs. The family generally used "Sister" instead of her name. Instead of "Patricia, go find Caroline" we would say, "Sister, go find Caroline."

Skat (Scat): Shouted out in a loud voice, used to scare off a cat. "SKAT, cat! Get away from my buttermilk bowl." But it can also be used as a short hand for "God Bless" when someone sneezes — this is one of those Southernisms that I don't explain: I just report. Instead of saying, "God Bless" when someone sneezes, you say: "Skat!" Some folks will say, "skat cat." I have no idea where the usage of this word came from, but I heard it as a young person many times. It drives non-Southerners crazy! They don't understand it, but what they don't realize is that we don't understand it either — we just accept it and enjoy blessing fellow Southerners when they sneeze, while, at the same time, confusing Yankees. Wow! It's a double blessing.

Skedaddle: What the Yankees did at the Battle of First Manassas (First Battle of Bull Run according to the Yankees or First Battle of Yankee Run according to me). To leave in great haste. "Ole Beauford *skedaddled* when he saw the revenuers *a-coming*."

Slap yo momma: Something so good, it would cause you to go crazy and dare to slap you mother — which, if she is a Southern mother, it would most likely be the last thing you do! *Back in the day*, the phrase was "slap yo mammy" which would have resulted in the same outcome! The word "mammy" was associated with the black lady hired to raise the children for rich white folks. It is one of those words that is no longer used in politically correct society.

Smiling like a possum eating briars: A pretended expression of happiness or an overly exaggerated smile. A possum eating thorny briars would not be smiling but grimacing in pain. Depending on the context and tone of the speaker's voice, it could mean either someone extremely happy with a large smile; someone sad with a pretended smile; or someone trying to fake being happy.

Smoking rope: "That boy was acting crazy! He must have been smoking rope." In the days of sailing ships, the rope used to set sails etc., on ships were made from fibers derived from hemp plants. Large fortunes were made growing hemp and providing it to rope-makers. Hemp has been used to make rope for thousands of years — some say as far back as 10,000 years. The leaves of the hemp plant are what today we refer to as marijuana. The hemp fibers contain a small amount of the same chemical marijuana leaves contain, but leaves contain it in much larger quantities. Often sailors would cut the rope and get a buzz smoking the rope. Hemp is still used today to make some ropes, but it is chemically treated to remove the "marijuana high" properties from the rope.

Snake in the grass: "Watch what you say around that man: he's a *snake in the grass.*" A snake in tall grass is hard to see. If you step on it, the snake will bite you. Some people give the impression that they are honest folks but will use any circumstance to stroke their ego (gossip) or unethically profit from another person's distress. Such folks are as harmful as an unseen *snake in the grass*.

Snow-ball's chance in hell: Extremely unlikely. "That boy don't have a *snow-ball's chance in hell* of turning into something good." Probability of success is zero!

So dumb; if he had an idea in his head, it would die of loneliness: Usually said in reference to a good ole boy who just made a silly or stupid mistake — especially if he has a track record of such choices or mistakes.

So dumb, he could not pour water out of a boot if the directions were written on the sole of the boot: Someone lacking basic common sense.

So ugly, that he had to tie pork chops to his legs just to get the dawgs to follow him around: One ugly dude! Dawg is Southern speak for dog.

So ugly, he (she) would make a freight train jump track and take off down a dirt road: Someone lacking personal appearance — bless his heart.

Sold down the river: This is a statement used to indicate ultimate betrayal by someone you considered a friend or someone you thought was motivated by honorable intentions. It dates back to times before *the War* when Yankees were gradually ending slavery in their states. Yankees never passed a law emancipating a slave alive at the time when that state's emancipation law was passed. What they did was pass laws declaring that when slaves who were born <u>after</u> the passage of their state's emancipation law reached a certain age (typically 18 to 21), that individual slave would be freed. But until that time, the Yankee slave-owner had full property rights to the slave's labor. The Yankee slave-owner worked his slaves until they approached the age of emancipation as established by the state's emancipation law. But before the slave reached the emancipation age, the Yankee slave owner would take the slave across the Ohio River and sell the slave to a slave trader. The slave trader would then ship the slave down river (Ohio River to Mississippi River) where the slave would be purchased to work on a plantation downriver. Instead of the promised freedom the slave was *sold down the river*, and there the slave would remain as a slave. Thus, the Yankee slave-owner cashed in on his capital investment in his slave property and helped to remove blacks from his state. Thus, the phrase *sold down the river*.

Something's the matter: There is a problem or issue but the details are not completely known. "Paw! Get yo gun. *Something's the matter* out in the hen house." Also used as an inquiry "What's the matter?"

Sot in his ways: Someone who is set in his ways. Some dictionaries associate the word with a drunkard or someone who drinks too much alcohol. I never heard it used as such—only as in set in his ways. "Uncle Frank was *sot in his ways*. He was not interested in any new *fandangle* way of doing things."

Southern Hospitality: The natural friendliness of most Southerners. In the South, hospitality is not a choice, it is a part of living among *kith and kin*. It boils down to basically following the Golden Rule we all learned in Sunday School "Do unto others as you would have them do unto you." Being a polite and helpful individual is a key characteristic of folks who personify *Southern hospitality*. Taking the time to say "yes or no, ma'am," "yes or no, sir," "please," and "thank you" distinguishes the rank and file Southerner from his Northern counterpart. Other attributes that contribute to *Southern hospitality* are lots of home cooking, kindness, helpfulness, charm, and charity.

Southern sugar vs Northern sugar: Sugar in the north is a white granulated sweetener, but sugar in the South means a kiss. Usually a kiss from a young grandchild given to grandfather. "Come over here, darling, and give yo granddaddy some sugar."

Spitting image: Looks like and acts like. That boy is the *spitting image* of his deddy (yes, it is pronounced the way it is spelled—deddy). He not only looks like (or *favors*) his deddy, but he acts like his deddy. The expression comes from an old English or *Scotch-Irish* saying, claiming that the son has his father's "spirit and image." Southerners shortened it to *spitting (spittin) image*. Can't explain why!

Squealed like a stuck pig: Someone who yelled out in pain or distress. Country boys who have had to "work on" young male animals to make the animal suitable for slaughtering will understand why the "stuck pig" is squealing.

Start an argument in an empty house: The type of person who would argue with a milepost. Someone who is greatly impressed by his own opinions and is generally disagreeable and argumentative with anyone who does not agree with him or her.

Stop that crying, or I'll give you some to really cry about: A stern warning given by Southern mothers to a child after he or she has been spanked. A little bit of crying is expected, but if it continues—usually the child's effort to complain about the spanking—mom will issue this warning, and surprisingly, the crying immediately ceases.

Supper: The last meal of the day. Incorrectly referred to by the uneducated or miseducated as dinner, which is the noon meal. Remember, the Lord Jesus had the Last Supper, not the Last Dinner.

Supreme federal government: The form of American government that was illegally (outside of the Constitution) established by Lincoln, the Republican Party, and their crony capitalist allies. It stands in contrast to the original, constitutionally limited, Republic of Sovereign States the Founding Fathers created and the Sovereign States ratified. States' Rights was reduced to states' privileges — exercised only if permitted by the *supreme federal government*.

Sweating like a field-hand in August: Wringing wet with sweat — sopping wet with sweat. This occurs when working outside in the summer and fall in the deep South. Perspiration (sweat) normally cools a person by evaporation, but when the humidity is 60% or above, very little evaporation occurs. The sweat beads upon the skin, and rolls down into the eyes, and soaks the *field-hand*'s shirt. *Field-hands* who are working their crops (planting, cultivating, or harvesting) face this every year. The harvesting of crops (picking cotton and pulling corn) begins in late August when temperatures get into the 90s and humidity is above 60%. I've been there and done that! When Donald and I complained to Dad about the heat, he told us to study hard, get a good job inside an air-conditioned office, and we would not have to work like *field-hands* when we are grown. Then he told us to quit complaining and get busy; we were wasting daylight. Modern folks call that "tough love," but we knew it as a reality — the daily struggle for survival in America's most impoverished region, the South. But in her destitution, we loved her all the more. The blood coursing through our veins descended from the blood of martyrs shed in the defense of our conquered, impoverished, and slandered people.

Sweet milk: Fresh milk. In the rural South before refrigeration, milk would not *keep* (not spoil) very long. It was drinkable for a short time. Fresh milk is the opposite of buttermilk.

Sweet tea: The essential drink served at *dinner* and *supper* in proper Southern homes. It is served cold, with lots of ice, and very sweet. Occasionally, mint and lemon are added. A jigger of bourbon is added for a late night "toddy."

Take a long walk off a short pier: The individual in question is a hindrance to polite society; a person who stands in the way of decent folks accomplishing a useful goal; generally speaking, someone society would be better off without, unless he repents of his ways and rejoins polite society. "We'd all be better off if that ole boy would *take a long walk off a short pier*." Our history has taught Southerners about the merciful application of forgiveness and redemption. Bad people can, with God's help, change their evil ways and rejoin civil society.

Tan yo hide: Southern mother issuing her last warning to a misbehaving child. "Johnny, if you dip your little sister's pigtails in the ink bottle again, I'm going to *tan yo* (your) *hide*," meaning that he is *fixing* to get a whupping (*whipping*).

Tarnation: An exclamation of surprise or consternation. "What in *tarnation* are Yankees doing in Atlanta? General Sherman did enough damage, but at least he did not hang around too long."

Tawk: Southern pronunciation for talk. "He's been *tawking* far too long."

That ole dog just won't hunt: A bad idea that will not work. When something is not useful for the purpose it was intended, it is as useless as a hunting dog that refuses to hunt. Also, a polite way of saying that something an individual just said or was reported to have said is less than truthful.

The deserving poor: People who through no fault of their own have fallen on hard times. They deserved the aid of their *kith and kin*. Aid is given with the aim of allowing them to, once again, become self-sufficient, productive, members of society. The only permanent welfare class allowed, *back in the day*, was that of widows, orphans, and the infirmed. To do otherwise was to encourage a parasitic life-style.

The loafers' bench: The bench in front of a country store. Both white and black Southerners often sat on the loafer's bench and visited with folks *a-coming* and a-going. It was a place for casual conversation where people *tawk* (talk) to each other. During the winter when it was too cold to sit outside, the pot belly wood-burning stove with chairs pulled around the stove substituted for *the loafers' bench*.

The past is never dead; it is not even past: This is a quote from the writings of Mississippi native and winner of the 1949 Nobel Prize for Literature, William Cuthbert Faulkner (1897-1962). It encapsulates the tradition loving South's attitude toward those permanent things handed down to us by our ancestors.

The pecking order: A dominance hierarchy in the chicken yard (see: *low peck hen*). In society it is similar to the military chain of command.

The Rebel Flag: The Battle Flag of the Confederate States of America, St. Andrews Cross, is often referred to as *the Rebel Flag*. In reality the first Rebel flag was the Thirteen-star, Betsy Ross flag used by George Washington and the American Colonies during the American War for Independence. See photos of Confederate flags in the center section.

The road to Hell is paved with good intentions: In social interaction, having good intentions is not enough. You must think through your potential acts to see if harm may result. The War on Poverty had good intentions, but the result has been a dramatic increase in black Americans living in single-parent households.

The South Shall Rise Again: A declaration uttered by partisan Southerners. Often as a joke or for its humorous impact, but also as an unconscious prayer. "Save your Confederate money boys! 'Cause *the South is going to rise again!*"

The Stars and Bars: The First National flag of the Confederate States of America. See photos of Confederate flags in the center section.

The War: Short term for The War for Southern Independence — when used as such the "w" is always capitalized. It is not just any war, but the most pivotal war in American history. It is the war that forcefully converted the original Constitutionally limited Republic of Sovereign States into a centralized supreme Federal Empire. The war that established the ruling political elites in Washington, D.C. as the final judge as to the limits, if any, of Federal powers, and, thereby, converted States' Rights into states' privileges. After Lincoln's victory over the Confederate States of America the Federal Empire evolved into the current Globalist Yankee Empire ruled over by the financial elites on Wall Street (crony capitalists), and the political elites in Washington, D.C. collectively known today as the "Deep State." *The War* brought about the merger of unlimited governmental power (the Federal government) and unlimited money (Wall Street elites who are underwritten by the Federal Reserve). See: *Civil War.*

They live so far back in the woods; they have to pipe the sunshine in and the moonshine out: Someone who lives far off the beaten track.

Throw a hissy fit: To have a temper tantrum usually over something insignificant in the greater scheme of things. "Mom threw a hissy fit when she found out that Sister used her good china."

Throw the baby out with the bath water: Doing harm when one was trying to do good. What has done more harm than the follies of the compassionate? Charity was provided originally by *kith and kin* and the church. It was provided to *the deserving poor* and only long enough for the recipient to "get back on his feet," i.e., be able to take care of himself. This type of charity encourages self-reliance, whereas unlimited charity as provided by government encourages dependency and social degeneration — government welfare is also a way in which leftist politicians can legally buy votes from an enlarged dependency class.

Thus-and-such: A generalized reference to a collection of nonspecific things or directions received. "He told us to do thus-and-such," she said while pointing to the project at hand.

'Til the cows come home: Expecting to be waiting for a long time.

Too big for his britches: This is applied to someone who thinks too much of himself and his opinions. Some would say he is a verbal bully. Too busy giving others his opinion and has no time to listen (and learn from) others. "Now that boy is just *too big for his britches*"

Too poor to paint, and too proud to whitewash: Bless their hearts, they are poor but proud. White wash was a cheap alternative to painting. Paint was expensive, so many folks substituted whitewash. But a whitewashed house was easy to identify—all your neighbors knew you could not afford to paint. Some folks caught in such a dilemma would let their house remain unpainted because they were *too poor to paint, but too proud to whitewash*.

Took-in: As in invited into family or home becoming part of your kith and kin. "Paw *took-in* his fourth cousin because he did not have a place to live." President Jefferson Davis and his wife, Varina, *took-in* Jim Limber, an orphaned black boy, and Jim became a part of the Confederacy's First Family, until he was kidnapped by the Yankees at the end of *the War*.

Tore up: Broken, destroyed or in a state of disrepair. You can't use that lawn mower—it's all "*tore-up*." When Southerners says something is "tore-up" they mean that it is broken or in a state of disrepair. When the term "*torn-up*" is applied to a person, it means the individual is in a state of emotional distress. "She is just all *torn-up* over the loss of her wedding band."

Tote: To carry. "Billy Jean, put that pone of corn-bread in a poke (paper bag), and *tote* it over to Aunt Vivian's house."

Truck farming: A fashion of farming typically engaged in by Southerners owning limited acreage. The truck farmer and his family raised various vegetables, harvested his crop, and took his produce to market. Vegetable crops raised by the truck farmer included cabbages, tomatoes, peas, butter beans, okra, and sweet corn. When harvested, the farmer loaded his "cash crop" (any crop raised to sell but not for personal consumption) on his truck and took it to market. Beginning in the 1930s, Southern states began improving rural roads, first gravel and then paved, to assist getting crops to market—the term "farm to market roads" is still used in some Southern states to indicate small rural roads.

Tump: To tip something over. "Be careful! You going to *tump* over the sweet milk."

Ugly, don't act ugly: Mind your manners, be polite and respectful of those around you. *Ugly* as used here does not refer to outward appearances but to the inner quality of the individual. Aunt Hattie Kennedy Smith told me once to be careful when deciding on which girl I want to marry because, *Pretty is as pretty does*. Another reference to inward beauty which trumps outward appearance.

Uncle Seth: A fictitious character created by Ron Kennedy and used to tell true stories about the War for Southern Independence. Uncle Seth's stories are all true; they were collected from written accounts in diaries, newspapers, and journals. All such accounts were originally written by Southerners who were participants in the events they recorded. The fictional *Uncle Seth* was based upon the personality of my Uncle Frank Smith. See, "Uncle Seth Fought the Yankees."

Unhappy as a rooster in an empty hen house: Someone lonesome and unhappy.

Uppity: Acting in a manner beyond your station in life. "He sure is acting *uppity* since he moved to the big city." Similar to someone who is *too big for his britches*.

Upside: Dramatic way of saying "on." "To get his attention, you'd have to hit him upside the head with a 2 by 4!" Why say you are going to hit someone on the head when it sounds more dramatic by saying you are going to hit them *upside* the head. Generally, when *upside* is used in this manner, it is more of a joke than a serious threat of physical violence — but not always.

Useful as a knot on a log or *a bump on a pickle*: Indicating uselessness, the individual is present in society, but he is serving no useful purpose. "That man is 'bout (about) as useful as a knot on a log." After World War II, the phrase "As useless as a screen door on a submarine" became another similar common expression.

Vae Victus: Latin meaning: "Woe to the vanquished." It was a term the Roman Empire used to describe what a conquered people could expect once they lost their freedom and became a captive nation within the Roman Empire. Today, the term is used by some Southern writers to describe the South after being conquered by the North.

Varmit: Southern word for varmint. A small animal, such as a mouse or a rat, that causes problems. Sometimes it is jokingly applied to small children. "Come here, you little *varmit*, and give granddaddy some *sugar*."

Waller around: What hogs do in a mud hole; they waller (wallow) around in it to cool off during the hot Southern summers. Can also be used to describe unkept people, "You *young'uns* (young children) stay away from those folks. They ant decent folks; they just *waller* around in their trash all day long."

We are getting down to the short rows: Close to being finished.

Well, I do declare: Surprised by something someone said or did. "*Well I do declare*! I didn't think that boy had enough sense to get in out of the rain."

Well, I reckon so: Same as saying "I suppose." Sometimes used as an exclamation of agreement with another speaker. Speaker one: "I don't care what the experts say, I'm not going to give up fried bacon." Speaker two: "*Well, I reckon so!*"

Well I'll be: An exclamation of surprise, often followed by "a monkey's uncle."

Well off: Financially well established. A freeholder owning his own land, home and not encumbered by debt.

Were you raised in a barn? Close the door! Usually said to children who do not realize that "I can't afford to air condition the whole neighborhood." Back in the day before air conditioning, it would be an admonition to close the screen door to keep the flies out.

What in Sam's hill: Bible-Belt way of saying "What the hell!"

Whichaway: Going in every direction at once. "Them Yankee Bummers scattered, when they saw General Forrest *acoming*. Yes sir! They ran every *whichaway*."

Whip: To whip someone. "If you don't hush yo mouth, I'm going to put a whipping on you!" Typically pronounced "whup."

Working from can to can't: Working from sun up to sun down. It can also refer to working extremely hard on a given project that has a definite deadline.

Yawl or Y'all (for the more formal, *you-all*): A handy little ole Southern pronoun. *Y'all* is a second person plural pronoun. It is non-sexist, referring to both males and/or females—as opposed to that horrid Yankee pronoun "you guys" used even when directed toward ladies. *Y'all* is a contraction of "you all." Although it is plural, it can also be used when speaking to an individual. "Hello, Jim Bob. How *y'all* doing?" Jim Bob, a good ole boy, intuitively understands that the speaker is asking about not only Jim Bob but his immediate family as well.

Yo: Southern synonym for "your." "Hush *yo* mouth, and mind *yo* own business!"

Yo mama and them: Almost exclusively New Orleans usage. It is similar to referring to an individual as *Y'all* when asking about the individual and his family.

Yonder, as in over yonder or down yonder: A general direction usually indicated by looking or pointing in the direction. If you ask how far, the reply will be, "Oh, just a little ways." If it is more than a little ways, the response will likely be, "Oh it's a fur piece but not much more that an axle greasing." Note: An "axle greasing" is the distance a horse drawn wagon could travel before you have to pull the wagon wheels and apply more grease. Horse drawn wagons wheels did not have ball bearings, and therefore, the wheels required re-greasing when used all day. An axle greasing is somewhere in the neighborhood of 20 to 30 miles.

You-all: More formal form of *yawl* or *y'all*.

You can't shackup with the devil and expect God to pay the rent: God will not spare you from the earthly consequences of your bad choices. God is not a get-out-of-jail-free card when it comes to the earthly consequences of bad choices.

You can't soar with the eagles if you stay up all night hooting with the owls: A typical Southern mother's warning to her children that partying all night may cause you to make bad grades in school or to lose your day job.

You kill your snakes, and I'll kill mine: A way of telling a nosey busy-body to mind his or her own business and leave you alone. Note: Snakes are viewed as being dangerous creatures that must be removed to protect small children and small domestic animals. Part of the dislike for snakes comes from the story of the fall of man in the Garden of Eden as recorded in the Holy Bible. Satan comes in the form of a serpent (snake) to tempt Eve. I have often watched my mother taking a hoe and killing a snake while declaring, "The ole devil himself trying to get in our house." The one exception is for a King snake. Dad always tried to protect King snakes because they kill other snakes. But even a King snake was not safe around Mom. I can still hear her telling Dad, "You'd better get that thing (King snake) away from here if you want it to live."

Young'uns: Young children. Some would say "kids" but rural folks know that kids refer to young goats; therefore, we would not refer to our *young'uns* as kids — unless you have some very strange looking *young'uns*.

Your chickens will come home to roost: Beware, because what you do away from home will find its way back to your mama. Free-ranging chickens will come back to their hen house to roost at night. We always counted our chickens late in the afternoon to make sure none were preyed upon during the day (by foxes, chicken-hawks or wild dogs). Southern mothers warned their children to be careful about how they act away from home because everyone knew each other, and word would get back if they did something to embarrass the family.

Your stomping ground: A person's stomping ground is the place where they are well known — a place they are familiar with. It comes from the Southern term "stomp-lot" (now days referred to as a feed lot) where the cattle would be fed and penned-up every night. Usually, it referred to your home and the general area in which you grew-up or where you now live. But don't think of your stomping ground strictly in a geographical sense. True, it is a place, but more importantly, it is a place where you know the people and the people know you. It is where you and your *kith and kin* live.

Lagniappe:

After unsuccessful efforts to take the Confederate capitol of Richmond, Virginia, an enraged Abraham Lincoln asked General (Winfield) Scott: "Why is it that in 1847 you were able to take Mexico City in three months with five thousand men, and we have been unable to take Richmond with one hundred thousand men?"

"I will tell you," said General Scott. "The men who took us into Mexico City are the same men who are now keeping us out of Richmond." Confederate Veteran Magazine, September 1913, page 471.

Karl Marx, an atheist, ridiculed religion as "the opiate of the masses." Southern scholar M. E. Bradford, PhD, declared that in our modern (politically correct, secular humanist) society it is not religion but the cult of equality that serves as the opiate of the masses. M. E. Bradford was a scholar, SCV member, and personal friend.

"What passes as standard American history is really Yankee history written by New Englanders or their puppets to glorify Yankee heroes and ideals," Grady McWhiney, PhD, Southern scholar and personal friend.

"The South contains the largest reservoir of Scotch-Irish blood in the whole world. Don't ever let anyone make you ashamed of your noble heritage," Rev. Robert Bradford, member of Parliament from Northern Ireland, and personal friend. Rev. Bradford was assassinated by the IRA in 1981.

"The system of (racial segregation) was born in the North and reached an advanced age before moving South in force," C. Vann Woodward, Southern scholar, Pulitzer Prize for History (1982).

Chapter 26:

EPILOGUE: THOUGHTS IN THE QUIET OF TWILIGHT

"THE TRIUMPHS OF might are transient—they pass and are forgotten—the sufferings of right are engraved deepest on the chronicle of nations." A Southerner wrote these lines shortly after the unfortunate results of the War for Southern Independence. In the face of triumphant evil and the war wreckage of his devasted Southern homeland, the Southern writer was even more convinced that *might does not make right.* Russian dissident Aleksandr Solzhenitsyn could have written the above-quoted lines. His book, "The Gulag Archipelago" (1974), describes the horrors inflicted upon innocent people by triumphant tyranny in the former Soviet Union. Yet, his book, written while he was one of the innumerable prisoners in the socialist Gulag—1958 to 1968—was the beginning of the end for Soviet Communism.

History is not a movie where the good guy always wins. Historic struggles are usually won by the strong. History teaches that evil men will use any means necessary to gain the strength necessary to win. Evil has its day, but evil eventually burns itself out and collapses. If we can learn anything from history, we should learn to avoid the tyranny of evil. But to avoid the tyranny of evil, we must first be a moral people who endeavor to avoid evil. Israel of old knew this, and for a while, it was a Godly nation, but slowly, generation after generation, the people abandoned Godliness and adopted the ways of the ungodly (secular) world. The people of ancient Israel wanted to be like the people in the rest of the world: they wanted to be accepted by the ungodly, they sought after the fleeting pleasures of the ungodly, and in the process, they rejected their nation's spiritual inheritance while adopting materialistic values of the secular world. They became weak spiritually. And weak spiritually, they became easy prey for those championing the tyranny of evil. They forgot that God instructed them to "Be ye separate" from the death producing world of material

*Father Ryan (1838-1886) Poet Priest of the Confederacy.
(Photo Wikipedia Commons).*

and secular pleasures. Today, the people of the *Bible-Belt* face a similar choice, the choice between spiritual wealth or the choice of the false glitter and temporary pleasures offered by the sinful secular humanist society that dominates America today. Remember Joshua's challenge to the Children of Israel as they entered the Promised Land, "Choose ye this day whom ye shall serve."

I remember Brother Douglas reading to our 5th-grade class Father Ryan's poem "A Land Without Ruins." No one understood it. We could not comprehend how there could be "glory in gloom," or how anyone could be proud of a land of ruins. As a youth, I did not

Epilogue

understand. It took a while, but I now understand and I hope, one day, my grandchildren and all the grandchildren of the South will understand.

"A Land Without Ruins," Father Abram J. Ryan, (circa 1880). The Poet Priest of the Confederacy. A dirge for a destroyed nation, and a lament for a conquered and oppressed people.

> Yes, give me the land where the ruins are spread,
> And the living tread light on the hearts of the dead;
> Yes, give me a land that is blest by the dust,
> And bright with the deeds of the down-trodden just.
> Yes, give me the land where the battle's red blast
> Has flashed to the future the fame of the past;
> Yes, give me the land that hath legends and lays
> That tell of the memories of long vanished days;
> Yes, give me a land that has story and song!
> Enshrine the strife of the right with the wrong!
> Yes, give me a land with a grave in each spot,
> And names in the graves that shall not be forgot!
> Yes, give me the land of the wreck and the tomb;
> There is grandeur in graves — there is glory in gloom;
> For out of the gloom future brightness is born,
> As after the night comes the sunrise of morn;
> And the graves of the dead with grass overgrown
> May yet form the footstool of liberty's throne,
> And each single wreck in the war-path of might,
> Shall yet be a rock in the temple of right.

It is only natural that a people who have been robbed of their future would cling to the memories of better days in their past. The past is not a place to live but a place of solitude and reflection, a place to discover which direction your life should take and a place to find the thrill and inspiration for a future yet unborn.

Deo Vindice.

Gerhard W. Heinsohn family at Willow Springs in Fayette County, TX circa 1940.

About the Author

RON AND HIS TWIN BROTHER DONNIE are the authors of the bestselling book *The South Was Right!* with more than 135,000 copies sold (2016). The Kennedy Twins have written five books together; their latest book together was *Punished with Poverty*. Ron authored *Reclaiming Liberty, Nullification: Why and How, Uncle Seth Fought the Yankees* and *Dixie Rising – Rules for Rebels*. Ron is past Division Commander, Louisiana Sons of Confederate Veterans (SCV), a life member of the Louisiana Division and the National SCV. He is a frequent speaker at SCV, Southern Heritage and other pro-Liberty groups.

Ron received a Master in Health Administration (MHA) from Tulane University in New Orleans, a Master of Jurisprudence in Health Law (MJ) from Loyola University in Chicago, and a Bachelor's degree from University of Louisiana Monroe. He retired in April 2015 after serving over 20 years as Vice President of Risk Management for a Louisiana based insurance company.

Books by James Ronald Kennedy

Dixie Rising—Rules for Rebels
Uncle Seth Fought the Yankees
Nullification: Why and How
Reclaiming Liberty

Books by The Kennedy Twins

Yankee Empire
Punished with Poverty
The South Was Right!
Why Not Freedom!
Was Jefferson Davis Right?
Nullifying Tyranny

Books by Walter Donald Kennedy

The Confederate Myth-Buster
Rekilling Lincoln
Lincoln's Marxists
Myths of American Slavery

Available From Shotwell Publishing

If you enjoyed this book, perhaps some of our other titles will pique your interest. The following titles are now available for your reading pleasure… Enjoy!

MARK C. ATKINS
WOMEN IN COMBAT
Feminism Goes to War

JOYCE BENNETT
MARYLAND, MY MARYLAND
The Cultural Cleansing of a Small Southern State

GARRY BOWERS
SLAVERY AND THE CIVIL WAR
What Your History Teacher Didn't Tell You

JERRY BREWER
DISMANTLING THE REPUBLIC

ANDREW P. CALHOUN, JR.
MY OWN DARLING WIFE
Letters from a Confederate Volunteer

JOHN CHODES
SEGREGATION
Federal Policy or Racism?

WASHINGTON'S KKK
The Union League during Southern Reconstruction

PAUL C. GRAHAM
CONFEDERAPHOBIA
An American Epidemic

WHEN THE YANKEES COME
Former South Carolina Slaves Remember Sherman's Invasion

JOSEPH JAY
SACRED CONVICTION
The South's Stand for Biblical Authority

SUZANNE PARFITT JOHNSON
MAXCY GREGG'S SPORTING JOURNALS 1842 - 1858

JAMES RONALD KENNEDY
DIXIE RISING: *Rules for Rebels*

WHEN REBEL WAS COOL

JAMES R. & WALTER D. KENNEDY
PUNISHED WITH POVERTY
The Suffering South – Prosperity to Poverty and the Continuing Struggle, 2nd ed.

YANKEE EMPIRE
Aggressive Abroad and Despotic at Home

PHILIP LEIGH
THE DEVIL'S TOWN
Hot Springs During the Gangster Era

U.S. GRANT'S FAILED PRESIDENCY

LEWIS LIBERMAN
SNOWFLAKE BUDDIES
ABC Leftism for Kids!

JACK MARQUARDT
AROUND THE WORLD IN EIGHTY YEARS
Confessions of a Connecticut Confederate

MICHAEL MARTIN
SOUTHERN GRIT
Sensing the Siege at Petersburg

SAMUEL W. MITCHAM
THE GREATEST LYNCHING IN AMERICAN HISTORY: *New York, 1863*

CHARLES T. PACE

LINCOLN AS HE REALLY WAS

SOUTHERN INDEPENDENCE. WHY WAR?
The War to Prevent Southern Independence

JAMES RUTLEDGE ROESCH

FROM FOUNDING FATHERS TO FIRE EATERS
The Constitutional Doctrine of
States' Rights in the Old South

KIRKPATRICK SALE

EMANCIPATION HELL
The Tragedy Wrought by Lincoln's
Emancipation Proclamation

KAREN STOKES

A LEGION OF DEVILS
Sherman in South Carolina

CAROLINA LOVE LETTERS

LESLIE R. TUCKER

OLD TIMES THERE SHOULD NOT BE FORGOTTEN
Cultural Genocide in Dixie

JOHN VINSON

SOUTHERNER, TAKE YOUR STAND!
Reclaim Your Identity. Reclaim your Life.

HOWARD RAY WHITE

HOW SOUTHERN FAMILIES MADE AMERICA
Colonization, Revolution, and Expansion From
Virginia Colony to the Republic of Texas 1607 to 1836

CLYDE N. WILSON

LIES MY TEACHER TOLD ME
The True History of the War for Southern
Independence & Other Essays

THE OLD SOUTH
50 Essential Books
(Southern Reader's Guide 1)

THE WAR BETWEEN THE STATES
60 Essential Books
(Southern Reader's Guide 2)

*RECONSTRUCTION AND
THE NEW SOUTH, 1865-1913*
50 Essential Books
(Southern Reader's Guide 3)

THE YANKEE PROBLEM
An American Dilemma
(The Wilson Files 1)

NULLIFICATION
Reclaiming the Consent of the Governed
(The Wilson Files II)

ANNALS OF THE STUPID PARTY
Republicans Before Trump
(The Wilson Files III)

JOE A. WOLVERTON, II

"WHAT DEGREE OF MADNESS?"
Madison's Method to Make
American STATES Again

WALTER KIRK WOOD

BEYOND SLAVERY
The Northern Romantic Nationalist
Origins of America's Civil War

GREEN ALTAR BOOKS
(Literary Imprint)

CATHARINE SAVAGE BROSMAN

*AN AESTHETIC EDUCATION
and Other Stories*

CHAINED TREE, CHAINED OWLS: Poems

RANDALL IVEY

*A NEW ENGLAND ROMANCE
and Other SOUTHERN Stories*

JAMES EVERETT KIBLER
TILLER

THOMAS MOORE
A FATAL MERCY
The Man Who Lost The Civil War

KAREN STOKES
BELLES
A Carolina Love Story

CAROLINA TWILIGHT

HONOR IN THE DUST

THE IMMORTALS

THE SOLDIER'S GHOST
A Tale of Charleston

GOLD-BUG
(Mystery & Suspense Imprint)

MICHAEL ANDREW GRISSOM
BILLIE JO

BRANDI PERRY
SPLINTERED
A New Orleans Tale

MARTIN L. WILSON
TO JEKYLL AND HIDE

Free Book Offer

Sign-up for new release notifications and receive a **FREE** downloadable edition of *Lies My Teacher Told Me: The True History of the War for Southern Independence* by Dr. Clyde N. Wilson and *Confederaphobia: An American Epidemic by Paul C. Graham* by visiting FreeLiesBook.com or by texting the word "Dixie" to 345345. You can always unsubscribe and keep the book, so you've got nothing to lose!

www.ingramcontent.com/pod-product-compliance
Lightning Source LLC
Chambersburg PA
CBHW020052170426
43199CB00009B/251